CUT THAT OUT

DR.ME

CUT THAT OUT

CONTEMPORARY COLLAGE
IN GRAPHIC DESIGN

CONTENTS

Introduction   006

Agnes Montgomery   008
Aliyah Hussain   012
Anna Beam   018
Anna Peaker   024
Atelier Bingo   028
Beth Hoeckel   034
Bill Kouligas & Kathryn Politis   038
Bráulio Amado   044
Cameron Searcy   048
Damien Tran   054
DR.ME   060
Ellery James Roberts   066
Hisham Akira Bharoocha   072
Hort   076
Hvass&Hannibal   082
Inge Jacobsen   088
Jelle Martens   094
Jesse Draxler   100
Joel Evey   106
John Powell-Jones   112
Jules Julien   116
Kustaa Saksi   122
Lee Noble   128
Leif Podhajský   134
Lewis McLean   140

Linda Linko   146
Louis Reith   152
Mario Hugo   158
Mat Maitland   164
Matthew Cooper   170
Matthew Craven   176
Merijn Hos   182
Michael Holland   188
Mike Perry   192
Mirko Borsche   198
MVM   202
Narcsville   208
Neasden Control Centre   214
Nick Mattan   218
Nous Vous   224
Paul Sahre   228
Robert Beatty   234
Ronny Hunger   240
Santtu Mustonen   246
Sebastian Haslauer   252
Stahl R   258
Stefan Sagmeister   264
Steve Hockett   270
Village Green   276
Yokoland   280

Artists' Websites   286

INTRODUCTION

RYAN DOYLE (DR)

My first encounter with collage was probably when my mum gave me a clip frame on my seventh birthday containing an assemblage of cut-out film photographs of me. Since then I have always enjoyed making and exploring the idea of collage. Its appeal is often its seemingly inherent accidental nature, which has fed into the heart of DR.ME's work. Most, if not all, our projects feature collage in some form, largely because our assignments frequently have a very short turnaround, requiring us to work intuitively, spontaneously and quickly, and still create something beautiful. With collage, you can make wonderfully surreal images with an infinite colour palette available at your fingertips. Over the years we have collected a vast array of cut-out books and magazines, off-cut papers and prints, discarded paintings and drawings, not to mention hundreds of copies of *National Geographic* ... it would be difficult to abandon the practice now.

MARK EDWARDS (ME)

While still at school, I was introduced by my mum to the son of one of her friends, Steve Smith. Steve, who chose to make work under the name of 'Neasden Control Centre', had recently graduated with a degree in illustration and had his newly published monograph under his arm. On being shown his book, everything suddenly came into focus for me. Images were layered using expressive illustrations; they were cut out, scanned in, redacted, blown up and shrunk down to give page after page of work that simply fascinated me. 'You get to do this for a living?' I asked. 'Yep,' he replied, and with that, I was hooked.

Georges Braque and Pablo Picasso coined the term 'collage' at the beginning of the 20th century to describe the technique of cutting and pasting elements of pre-existing images or text and then rearranging them to create an entirely new image. Just as a painter selects his paint or a carpenter her tools, collage artists use components of their own choosing and mixed media to create brand new images that often bear little semblance or relationship to the original sources.

After collage's introduction into the mainstream art world by Picasso and Braque, artist Kurt Schwitters began to experiment with the medium as early as the start of the 1920s, using wood in his creations. Collage gained even more exposure during the pop art movement after artistic giants such as Andy Warhol, Robert Rauschenberg and Richard Hamilton used it in some of their large-scale pieces. Throughout the 1960s, collage also appeared in advertising and music packaging – one famous example is Peter Blake's album cover for *Sgt. Pepper's Lonely Hearts Club Band* by The Beatles. This trend would continue until the present day: Tsunehisa Kimura's part-apocalyptic, part-Surrealist *The City Welcomes a Fresh Morning* (see opposite) was used on the cover of Cut Copy's 2011 album *Zonoscope*.

Collage today is a very broad term and can no longer be considered simply cut-and-paste. It can encompass assemblage, photomontage, mixed-media installation, digital manipulation or painting. More and more creatives are combining various media and methods in the search for something that has never been seen before. They are reluctant to be pigeonholed into one specific way of working and their approaches are far more multidisciplinary, which often leads to wild and unexpected results. The resurgence of collage in the last decade has not only led to more experimental personal work, but commercial work as well. Although collage has existed as an art form for considerably longer, the arrival of the Internet and social media has helped it to gain unprecedented popularity.

Cut That Out celebrates fifty international creative studios or individuals for whom collage is a key component in their work. From traditional cut-and-paste methods to contemporary digital collage and even tapestry and video, we show some of the most innovative uses of collage today and ask whether its definition has changed since the days of Braque, Picasso and their 20th-century successors. Certainly, collage doesn't have to be limited now to cut-and-paste methods. It can be three-dimensional; digitally augmented; screen-printed; paper mixed with paint; ink mixed with photography. In the following pages, we question the creatives on their individual techniques and processes, sources of inspiration and thoughts on the medium.

The creative studios in this compendium have made visuals for an extraordinary range of clients, including Nike, American Express, Sony PlayStation and *The New York Times*. Collage was once considered a very intimate, personal medium: there is evidence that Victorian families would create photomontages for display in their homes. Fast-forward to the 21st century, and international companies are approaching creatives directly for magazine covers, packaging, advertising and record sleeves, which is testament to the power of collage as a means of communication. This book shows the difference between creating a collage for yourself and creating one according to a strict brief, especially in light of the general perception of collage as such a naturally spontaneous and unpredictable art form.

Both the commercialization of collage and the ongoing discovery of new techniques mean that contemporary collage has evolved well beyond cutting out pictures and glueing them to a piece of paper. Hence the different studios' work varies drastically – and intentionally so. In effect, this book is a kind of collage – a wild collection of conflicting artistic sensibilities, formats and approaches – all brought together by a common appreciation for collage in its various guises.

Tsunehisa Kimura, TOSHI WA SAWAYAKANA ASA WO MUKAERU (*The City Welcomes a Fresh Morning*)
from *Kimura Camera: Tsunehisa Kimura's Visual Scandals by Photomontage* (Parco, 1979)

AGNES MONTGOMERY

Philadelphia-born Agnes Montgomery creates work that typically features psychedelic or carnivalesque landscapes: worlds where children play in swimming pools alongside tigers and koala bears. A self-taught artist, her collages are made by hand using found paper, small scissors and a magnifying lamp.

Montgomery's work has appeared on many artists' record sleeves, but perhaps most notable is the work she created for experimental musician Panda Bear (see following pages). In these works, her Surrealist collage creations, with their juxtaposition of unrelated elements, match perfectly with the multi-layered, experimental pop music. Along with the work she creates for the music industry, Montgomery has exhibited her collages around the world, including New York and Philadelphia. For these exhibitions, she scans and enlarges the collages in order to print in a large format on canvas.

'BROS' SINGLE COVER from the album *Person Pitch* by Panda Bear (Paw Tracks). Collage on paper, 2007

POOL PARTY, album cover for *Person Pitch* by Panda Bear (Paw Tracks). Collage on paper, 2007

In terms of sourcing your imagery, which materials are you drawn to?
I like old magazines – I find them at flea markets or garage sales.
There is something about the tactility of the paper and the weight
of them, as well as the surprise of what I might find when turning the
pages. It's a bit of a mission to do this without knowing what I am
looking for, but the outcomes are limitless and often surprising.

Do you then prefer to work digitally or by hand?
I don't even know how to make a collage digitally. I never learned
how to use Photoshop or any such program. It would probably come
in handy some time but I'm not that attracted to the idea of moving
images around on a computer screen, so I've put off learning how to do
it. I like using my hands – being able to sift through drawers and boxes
of paper cut-outs and lay them out on tables and shift them around.
It can be done anywhere and with very few tools; I prefer to work with
minimal glue and limited mess or smell – just lots of bits of paper like
confetti all over the floor. It feels both fast and immediate, but maybe
that's just because I haven't learned the digital way. Working by hand,
I don't have the convenience of erasing or altering part of an image
or making things look uniform and perfect, but perhaps I prefer the
challenge of seeing what I can do solely with what I have.

Do you prefer making collages in the traditional way or do you like to
experiment with other forms of collage or media?
So far I have never really done a project involving mixed media – I still
enjoy handling pictures on little pieces of paper. I have created several
découpages, though: images stuck on top of chocolate boxes and on
an old large trunk – that sort of thing.

'CARROTS' SINGLE COVER from the album *Person Pitch*
by Panda Bear (Paw Tracks). Collage on paper, 2007

'I'M NOT' / 'COMFY IN NAUTICA' SINGLE COVER from the album
Person Pitch by Panda Bear (Paw Tracks). Collage on paper, 2007

Were your collages that appear on the Panda Bear record covers made
especially for the project or had you made them previously?

Noah Benjamin Lennox (otherwise known as the musician Panda Bear)
really liked the collages I was making at the time and asked if I would
like to make some new ones for his record. I made a collage for each
song on the *Person Pitch* record, and they were released as vinyl singles
before the full-length album appeared. Noah had the initial idea of using
collage for the visuals on the record, mirroring the music itself, which
is a kind of collage of sample material. Being good friends with him, I
knew it would be a fun collaboration, but I became very inspired as soon
as I heard the songs. After *Person Pitch* I then made the artwork for the
record *Evenfall* by my husband Sebastien Schuller, along with a tour
poster and a T-shirt.

When did you first start making collages?

During my early childhood, my mother and I had fun cutting out pictures
from mail order catalogues, glueing them on top of envelopes and
making our own cards to send to family and friends at holiday times.
We would use flowers from seed catalogues or animals from zoo
pamphlets, or in fact any kind of advertisement or junk mail. We always
had a drawer to sift through when the time came to make a collage. We
often made Valentine cards for my classmates, and my mother made me
'welcome home' collages after I returned from summer camp. Collage
wasn't just something I did during my childhood – it was something
I kept up in my teens, cutting up fashion magazines and making my
own scrap books, or even making little collages to go on the insert of
mix cassette tapes to exchange with friends. It was always an easy and
fun way to be creative. In my twenties I was more into making jewellery
and mosaics, which are similar in some ways to making collages. Later
on I saw a gallery show of Joseph Cornell collages in New York. I was
familiar with his box assemblages with cut-out pictures pasted inside
and always liked them, but I didn't know he had also made collages.
They inspired me to restart my hobby and cut and paste some more.

ALBUM COVER FOR *EVENFALL* by Sebastien Schuller (PIAS France). Collage on paper, 2009

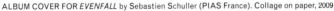

ALIYAH
HUSSAIN

Aliyah Hussain is based at the Islington Mill studios in Salford, UK, where she creates a wide variety of collage-based works, including poster art, screen prints and costumes. An eclectic blend of photography, painting, printmaking and performance, Hussain's multidisciplinary practice enables her to create pieces in which references to futurist narratives and utopian visions clash with retro aesthetics and DIY techniques.

Hussain has worked on a wide variety of projects, from art-directing the Sounds From The Other City festival to commissioned artworks for Yuck Print House and the tape label Sacred Tapes. Her pieces have been exhibited at the Saatchi Gallery in London and throughout Manchester, and in 2009 she received the Google Photography Award.

JOLLIES I, personal project made during residency at La Escocesa in Barcelona. Vinyl stickers on a photograph, 2013

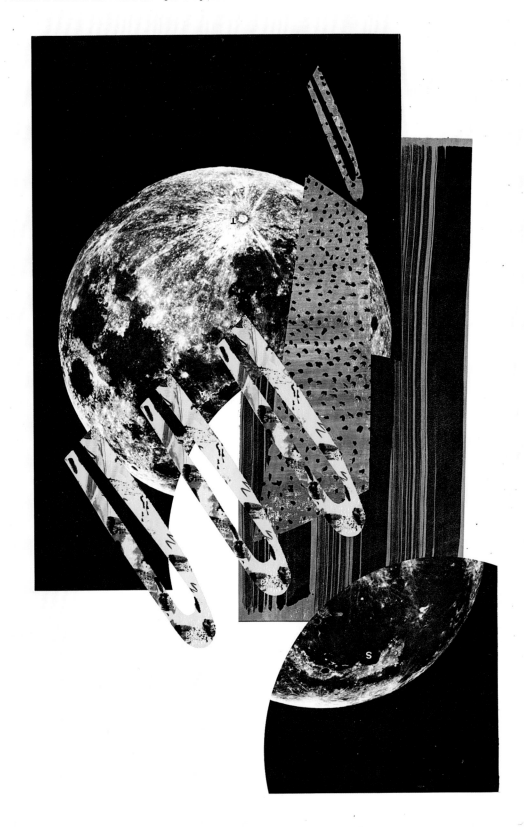

ALIYAH HUSSAIN

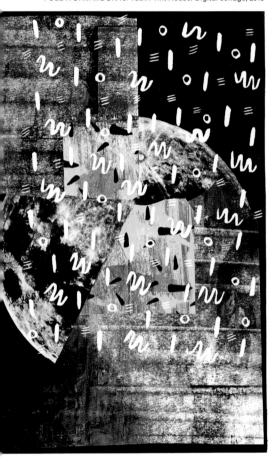

FULL WORM MOON for Yuck Print House. Digital collage, 2015

When did you first come across collage?
Most likely when studying Dada in college. I also remember first coming across the work of Hannah Höch and being blown away.

Since your first exposure to Hannah Höch, have any other collage-based artists stood out for you?
I really love everything Atelier Bingo [see page 28] produce. Although a lot of their works are screen prints rather than straight-up collages, there is always a sense that every element of the composition was made intuitively and by chance. They use bold, simple, roughly cut shapes that embody the collage aesthetic and approach. It's just so satisfying to look at. I also love the entire poster and record cover work by Alex Humphreys. Her approach is similar to Atelier Bingo's, but the outcome is completely different: it is both wild and unpredictable.

What is the appeal of collage for you?
I get a kind of buzz off of it. It's such an immediate process, and I tend to work quite intuitively, churning out works quickly, which I find very satisfying. Placed within the context of my wider practice, I use collage as something in between a meditation and a puzzle to solve. I see my sculptural and installation work as physical collage, so the works on paper are essentially exercises in preparation for the physical, object-based works. Overall I'm also interested in the juxtaposition of things that don't traditionally go together. I like to think about the endless possible combinations of different elements ... there's a certain sense of freedom in knowing something will never be repeated.

When it comes to sourcing these different original elements, how do you select which materials to use?
Most of the imagery I use is my own. I take a lot of photographs and have done for a number of years, so I like to look back into my archive and use those as source materials. I also recycle old drawings that didn't quite make the cut first time around. More recently I have been screen-printing large blocks of swirled-up colour onto paper and then working on them further using ink and mark-making. I like the illusion of depth this gives, and it also adds layers in terms of the number of processes that are being used. When a single piece of material used within a collage has had lots of work put into it, then this means I can be a bit more sparse and minimal with composition and arrangement. I like to let the pieces speak for themselves.

Do you prefer to make collages digitally or by hand?
I work using a mixture of both; I'm forever trying to find a balance between the two. At the moment I am aiming for more complexity in my handmade work and more simplicity in my digital work, as I naturally do the opposite. Working digitally, the combinations are endless and you can get far too wrapped up in a composition, trying things over and over. Sometimes it can end up quite mathematical and I lose track of what I originally set out to do. But on the other hand there can be a great deal of freedom working digitally. You can craft a shape or overall piece out of something an endless number of times and distort it so it becomes something unrecognizable. If I wanted to do the same with the handmade pieces it would take forever and require lots of planning. Having said that, working by hand, there is something interesting in knowing I've got one shot at a particular piece. It means there is a higher rate of failure, but the experience of failure also results in the discovery of new ideas.

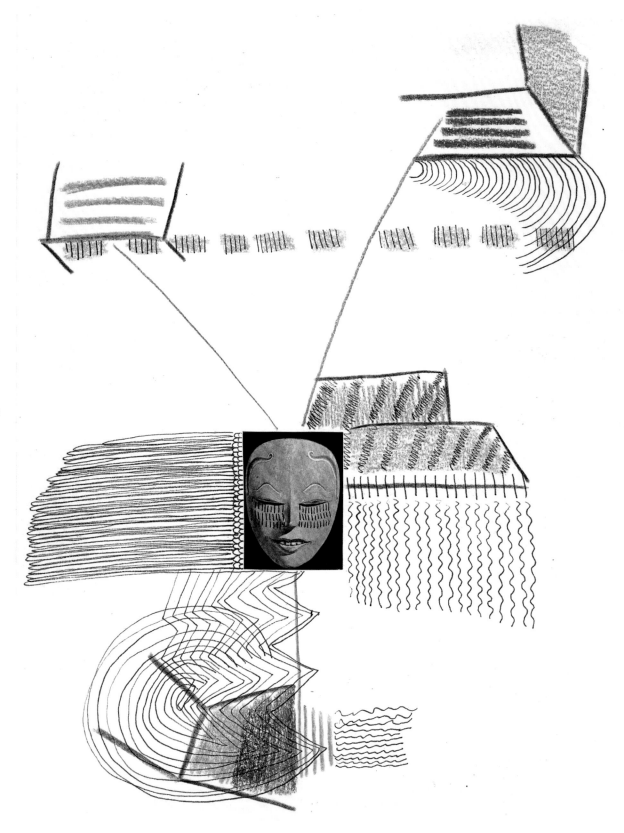

FULL WORM MOON for Yuck Print House. Collage on paper, 2015

FULL WORM MOON for Yuck Print House. Digital collage and found imagery, 2015

SPRING MOON for Yuck Print House. Digital collage, 2015

SPRING MOON for Yuck Print House. Digital collage, 2015

ANNA BEAM

Originally from Baltimore, Maryland, Anna Beam now runs her own creative studio in east London, where she creates collage-based pieces for clients such as Cloudwater Brew Co. She is also a freelance prop-maker and hand-embroiderer. Beam's work centres on combinations of patterns and colours, as well as bringing together various different forms of media – cut and painted paper, thread and occasionally ceramics – to create an overall effect that is both visually striking and highly textural. In addition to her 2-D creations, Beam co-founded the multi-disciplinary collective Volkov Commanders along with fellow graphic designers Aliyah Hussain (see page 12) and Mariel Osborn. Together they have directed and performed in live immersive events, workshops and music videos.

UNTITLED, personal project. Gouache and paper collage, 2013

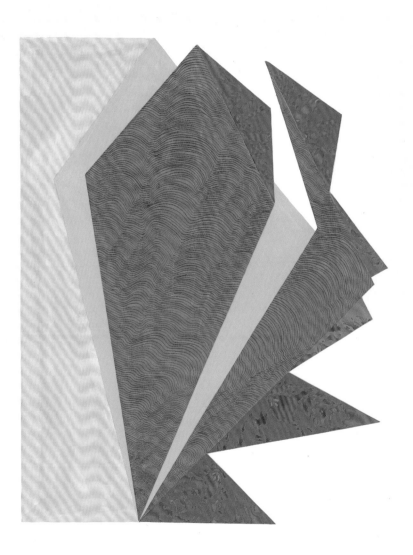

LAKESIDE, personal project. Coloured pencil and gouache on paper, 2013

UNTITLED, part of the *Circle Series* project. Paper collage, 2014

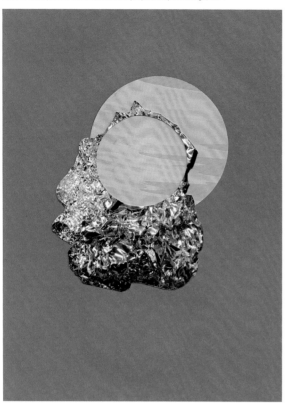

UNTITLED, part of the *Circle Series* project.
Paper collage, 2014

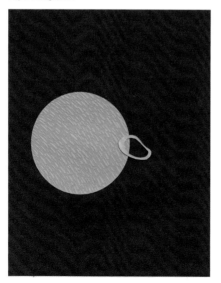

Which materials do you use to make your collages?
Most of my collages come from scraps and offcuts from other projects, or from failed work that I've then cut up.

What's the most unusual thing you've included in a collage?
My final piece at art school was this big, scrolling collage done directly onto a wall. It incorporated plastic, cloth, wire and probably some other stuff. It was certainly busy. Now, though, I don't really use anything 'unusual', but I do apply the same methods of working with paper to my surface pattern and product design work. For example, the bags I make are decorated using a combination of screen printing, embroidery, beading and appliqué. I try to keep the process of making them as intuitive and spontaneous as my work with paper.

Is it the tactility of the collage-making process that draws you to it?
I really love the physicality and the inherent improvisation in making collages. It's a nice contrast to my other work, which is often slow and laborious. Making collages helps me make 'accidental' discoveries about colour and form, which I then take and use in my other work. For me there's always an element of surprise, and I am often most happy with the ones that were totally unplanned. I like to think of it as though my hands are messing around while my brain has its back turned. It keeps things interesting!

I guess, then, that you prefer to work by hand as opposed to digitally?
Yes, by hand, although I'm starting to use a combination of both, as I find that it adds another layer of surprise and possibility to the process, as well as making it feasible for me to turn stand-alone pieces into designs for surface pattern, etc.

Do you remember your first contact with collage?
I don't know when I first came across collage as an art form, but it is something I remember doing a lot as a teenager. Though back then my collages came in the form of scrapbook pages filled with pictures of my friends, mishmashed together with newspaper clippings, doodles and whatever other weird bits of detritus I thought were interesting at the time.

Do you have an all-time favourite piece of collage?
It's always changing, but right now my mind goes immediately to Matisse and the collages he did in his later years. Maybe it's a cop out to go straight to the 'big boys', but there you go. I'm always interested in other people's creative processes, and what I love about that body of work is the life, freshness and spontaneity that he was able to achieve despite the fact that, when you see these works in person, all the tiny pin holes in each piece of paper indicate that Matisse took a great deal of careful consideration over their placement.

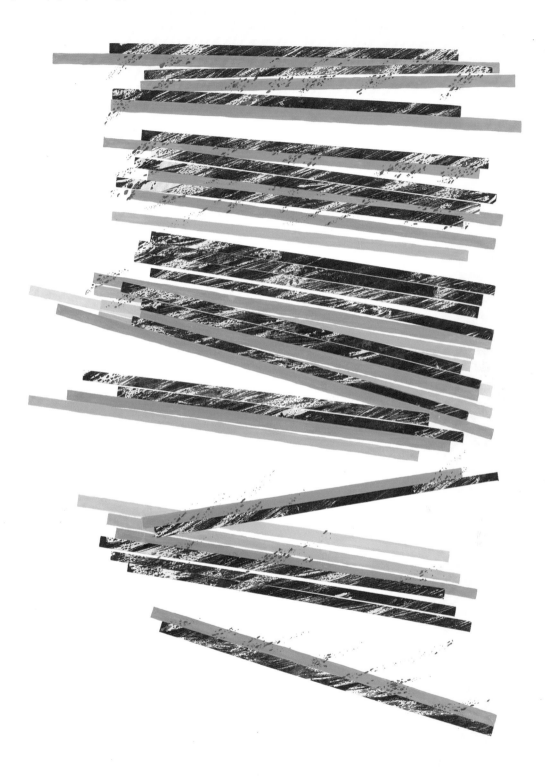

UNTITLED, personal project. Paper collage, 2014

Opposite: UNTITLED, personal project. Paper collage, 2014

ANNA BEAM

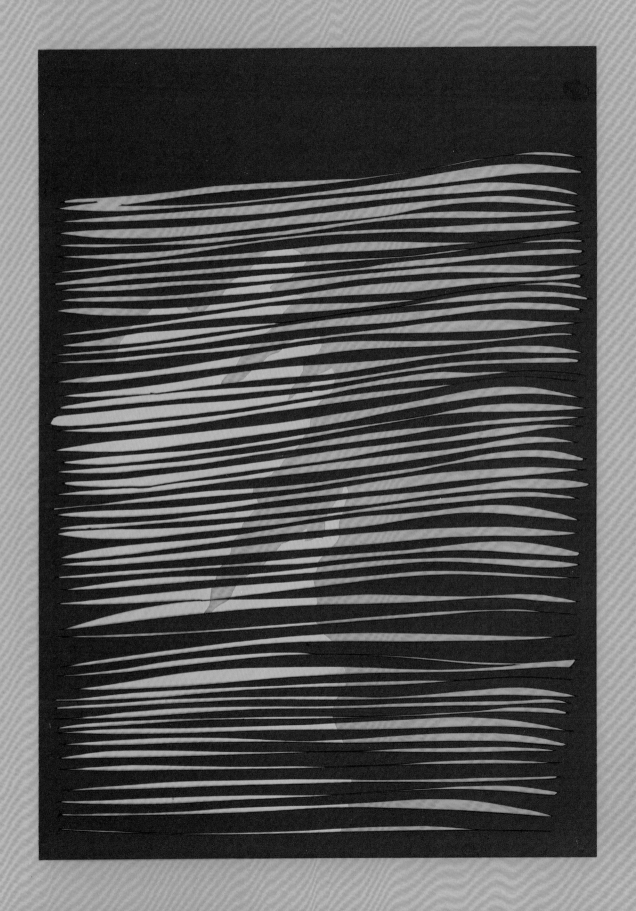

ANNA PEAKER

Anna Peaker is a Leeds-based graphic artist who has worked on record covers, tape packages and posters for a range of musicians and record labels including The Tetleys, Soft Power Records and Too Pure Records. She has also had exhibitions held in the UK and US.

Peaker's aesthetic is sultry, pared-down and minimalist, with each design sticking closely to its own, often monochromatic, chosen colour palette. She draws attention to the negative space surrounding the subject images by allowing these images' various, more intricate elements to exist harmoniously, as shown in her record sleeve design for The Wharves (see page 26). Often, she also shows a similar level of restraint by visually isolating each element (see below and page 27).

WINDOWS, personal project. Digital collage, 2013

ANNA PEAKER

POSTER FOR MELT BANANA GIG. Digital collage, 2012

Why do you think collage is an apt medium for your practice?
My work has a lot to do with composition and experimenting with placement of images. I'm interested in symbology within imagery and how ideas can be communicated when these symbols interact with one another, and collage is the perfect medium to explore this.

When did you first realize collage was something that interested you artistically?
Apart from cutting stuff out of catalogues and glueing them onto bits of paper when I was a child, I supposed I recognized it as an art form through looking at record sleeves as I grew up. I remember being particularly drawn to my mum's copy of *Revolver* by The Beatles when I was little (she didn't have *Sgt. Pepper's Lonely Hearts Club Band*). Indeed, I'm now obsessed with black and white!

Where do you tend to source imagery from?
Anywhere, really – old books, magazines, postcards. For instance, I have these old postcards of women dressed up as Greek mythological figures that I've used before. If I'm looking for an image of something more specific I will try and hunt it down online.

Have you ever used anything unusual in a collage?
I think the unusual occurs when you combine certain images. You may have the most mundane everyday image, but when it's put together with something else that conflicts with it, the overall effect is almost otherworldly.

Do you prefer to work digitally or by hand?
I'm going to have to say digitally, because it allows you to have more precision and control.

Do you have a favourite piece of design or illustration that uses collage?
It's hard to pick just one. There are many artists and designers that I admire who use collage in their work – Tadanori Yokoo, Toyen, Sätty, Karel Vaca and Linder to name just a few.

RECORD SLEEVE FOR *AT BAY* by The Wharves (Gringo Records). Digital collage, 2014

ATELIER BINGO

A collaboration between artists Maxime Prou and Adèle Favreau, Atelier Bingo is a creative studio based in Saint-Laurent-sur-Sèvre, France. Its clients range from publications such as *Vogue* and *Wanderlust Travel Magazine* to Sosh: City Guide app and Calepino, a stationery company.

The studio's love for experimental screen printing is underpinned by its use of cut-and-paste collage work, which is beautifully reminiscent of and draws inspiration from Henri Matisse's *Cut-Outs*. Rather than simply creating an image and printing it, they build it up, colour by colour, meaning they will only know what the piece looks like when the final colour or element is added.

POSTER FOR 'NEW FRONTIERS' at the Publishing Innovation Conference. Handmade collage and screen print, 2015

J'AI UN THERMOS DANS MA POLO, personal project. Handmade collage and screen print, 2015

ICEBERG MINIMAL, personal project. Handmade collage and screen print, 2015

BLUE FLORAL ABSTRACT for *Wrap* magazine. Handmade collage and screen print, 2014

Overleaf: LA CHASSE AUX COYOTES, personal
project. Handmade collage and screen print, 2015

When did you first come across collage?
  Adèle: When we started Atelier Bingo in 2013. Maxime and I realized
  we shared a very similar artistic spirit and identity, which naturally
  led to us cutting paper together.

Do you have a favourite piece of design or illustration that uses collage?
  Maxime: 'Hamster Girl' by Marnie Weber, which appeared on the album
  cover for *A Thousand Leaves* by Sonic Youth in 1988.
  Adèle: Malin Gabriella Nordin's collages – I love all of them.

From where do you tend to source your images?
  Maxime: We just use plain coloured paper with no print or pattern on
  it. We buy it everywhere. Regarding our sources of inspiration, it's more
  complicated as we work as a duo. In one sense, I suppose this makes
  it easier for us to generate work. If one of us is out of ideas and doesn't
  want to start off the creative process, she can continue to choose
  coloured paper while the other sets to work. We are continually inspired
  by combinations of colours, shapes, comics, music, vintage stuff, dogs,
  supermarkets, grapefruit, cultural traditions and course lists.

Does the process ever unearth any surprises for you?
  Adèle: We like using the shapes that we didn't consider using at the
  beginning of the process, such as the off-cuts.

Do you prefer to make collages digitally or by hand?
  Maxime: By hand, of course, but digital can be better for work with clients
  (for clothes, decoration, etc). We always make sure to scan our shapes
  of paper for the purpose of creating a digital collage afterwards.

POSTCARD COLLECTION, personal project. Handmade collage and screen print, 2015

BETH HOECKEL

Beth Hoeckel is a multidisciplinary artist from Baltimore, Maryland. Having previously studied painting, photography and printmaking at the School of the Art Institute of Chicago, she creates collages and mixed media for a number of clients, including *The Atlantic Magazine*, *BUST Magazine* and *Condé Nast Traveller*.

Thematically, Hoeckel's work is about losing touch with reality; about getting lost in a daydream. In many of her works, she also shows people's interactions with and reactions to the power of nature. Collage is always an integral part of her creations, whether she is creating abstract paintings, ink drawings or book covers. The materials she uses also vary enormously – she has previously incorporated liquid acrylics, india ink and gouache into her work.

RECORD SLEEVE FOR *SINGLES* by Future Islands (4AD). Hand-cut collage, 2014

BETH HOECKEL

When did you first start making collages?
I don't believe I ever made a conscious effort to start doing collages; it came to me instinctively and it's been part of my style for a long time – ever since I was in high school. I've always been drawn to old photographs and books and I started keeping a collection of them when I was a teenager.

Why do you think that this attraction naturally developed?
One person's trash is another person's treasure. I love the idea of reclaiming old materials and appropriating their original meaning, giving them an entirely new context. I have magazines that are sixty years old or older that are still vibrant and beautiful, and I love to repurpose their images to create a dream-like environment that is formed from the realities of our world but reconstructed to appear surreal.

Do you mostly source your original material from magazines?
Almost all of my material comes from vintage publications ranging from the 1950s to the 1970s. Occasionally I use older imagery but, visually speaking, my favourite era is the mid-1950s.

Do you have a preference for working by hand as opposed to digitally?
I do prefer handmade. I have nothing against working digitally, but it just doesn't fit in with my particular style so the results tend to feel quite unnatural.

Do you use exclusively paper materials?
I use mainly paper, but on rare occasions something unusual finds its way in. It might be hair, thread, scraps of fabric, a used tea bag or a coffee stain.

PHOTO SYNTHESIS, personal project. Collage on paper, 2011

BETH HOECKEL

BILL KOULIGAS & KATHRYN POLITIS

Bill Kouligas and Kathryn Politis are Berlin-based graphic designers who have worked together since the inception of Kouligas's record label, Pan, in 2008. At the start they had a very clear-cut concept and aesthetic for the label: a series of ten music releases whose covers consisted of found black-and-white images which were then overlaid with geometric designs that were silk-screened in colour on a transparent PVC sleeve. Although afterwards these guidelines became less prescriptive, the general idea of the silk-screened PVC sleeve featuring some form of typography and geometrical shapes and lines remains. There is also an emphasis on layers – the duo's central concern is to have the artwork indicate depth, hinting at the multidisciplinary nature of the label's aim to combine art and music.

RECORD SLEEVE FOR *ESSTENDS-ESSTENDS-ESSTENDS* LP by Ben Vida (Pan Records). Handmade, layered collage, 2012

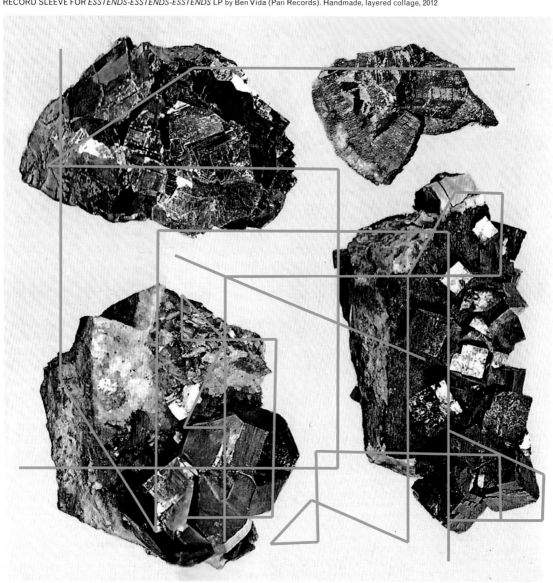

BILL KOULIGAS & KATHRYN POLITIS

RECORD SLEEVE FOR *IMPOSSIBLE SYMMETRY* LP by Helm
(Pan Records). Handmade, layered collage, 2012

When did you first come across collage?
[Bill Kouligas and Kathryn Politis]: Collage – its form and aesthetics
– has been firmly embedded within the visual language of our
environment for as long as we can remember. It has simply become
a natural feature within our surroundings: one that we have all
become accustomed to experiencing.

What do you think is the attraction of collage?
The tension and energy that results from juxtaposing clashing images
is interesting. The idea, too, that you can create endless new meanings
and messages from multiple images, references and angles all point
to this notion of the medium as a visual language. Today, appropriation
is inevitable. It is inherent within communication.

Do you have a favourite piece of design that uses collage?
In late 2015, Dutch artist Harm van den Dorpel launched *Deli Near
PAN Franchise (Autosurfing) β*, a division of an online project called
Deli Near. This is an algorithm that maps decaying actor-network
theory visuals across the VW Dome and it is open for anyone to
upload material.

From where do you tend to source your images?
The images we choose come from various sources depending on the
job at hand and the context behind it. Some of them are found in old
publications and a lot are found online. Many of the images are also the
results of our collaborations with other photographers, or they even
come from the musicians or artists on the label [Pan Records].

Do you prefer to make collages digitally or by hand?
We have no preference. The method really depends on the context –
it is a part of the design process. Sometimes artwork calls specifically
for a handmade feel and sometimes vice versa – the method or effect
is essentially a part of the image.

RECORD SLEEVE FOR *VIDÖPPNA SÅR* LP by Sewer Election
(Pan Records). Handmade, layered collage, 2010

RECORD SLEEVE FOR *REPAS FROID* LP by Ghédalia Tazartès (Pan Records). Handmade, layered collage, 2011

BILL KOULIGAS & KATHRYN POLITIS

RECORD SLEEVE FOR *DANCE CLASSICS VOL.III* LP by NHK'Koyxen (Pan Records). Collage on paper, 2013

RECORD SLEEVE FOR *DANCE CLASSICS VOL.II* LP by NHK'Koyxen (Pan Records). Collage on paper, 2012

RECORD SLEEVE FOR *DANCE CLASSICS VOL.I* LP by NHK'Koyxen (Pan Records). Collage on paper, 2012

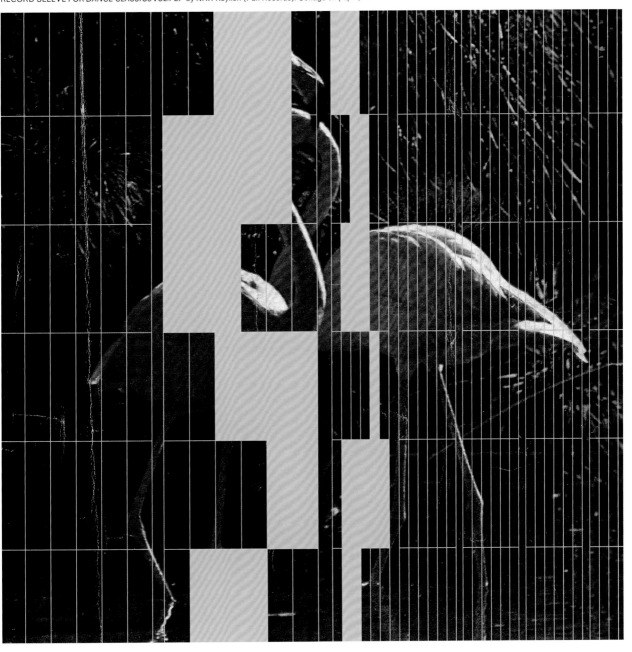

43

BILL KOULIGAS & KATHRYN POLITIS

Bráulio Amado is a graphic designer from Almada, Portugal, who now lives and works in New York. He splits his time between working as a designer for *Bloomberg Businessweek* and creating posters for bands and musicians including Hot Chip, Suuns and William Basinski.

Whereas Amado's work for *Bloomberg Businessweek* tends to rely largely on humour, directness and immediacy to convey its message and grab people's attention, his concert posters often demand multiple viewings. Similar to the psychedelic posters in the 1960s, Amado plays heavily with typography, often making it almost illegible so that the viewer has to stop and decipher what is written.

POSTER FOR HOT CHIP (DJ SET) at Good Room, New York. Digital collage, 2015

Opposite: POSTER FOR GREYS at Little League Shows. Digital collage, 2014

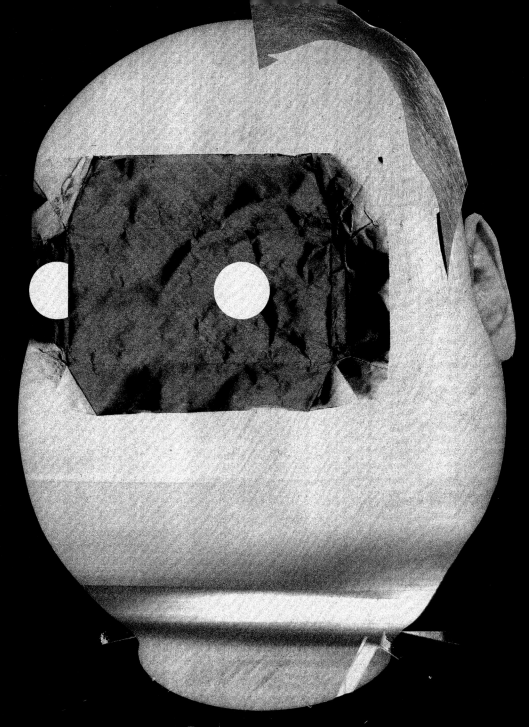

LITTLE LEAGUE SHOWS
THIRSTY & MISERABLE
PRESENT:

06.GREYS
11.

SCHOKOLADEN   ACKERSTR.169

DOORS 7PM   SHOW 8PM

I HAVE NO MOUTH
AND I MUST SCREAM

When did you first start making collages?
I think I made my first punk zine when I was 16 – it looked terrible. But it did make me start playing with collages.

Do you have a favourite collage?
Growing up with the hardcore Punk scene, the whole collage aesthetic was always something that influenced me. All of the zines my friends did back then were beautiful pieces of design because … well, they had no idea what they were doing design-wise, but it was fun and it felt natural. My favourite collage works came from the band Black Dice. The artwork just connected so well with their sound, which was in itself a kind of collage – a sample of weird, crazy noises and songs.

What attracts you to the medium of collage?
I really like the process of having two different images and then messing them up in order to tell a totally different story. When I draw, I'm creating my own universe in my own style. With collage it's more about solving a puzzle; playing with different pieces and trying to figure out what you can do with them.

How do you go about this process of making a collage? Do you work digitally or by hand?
Handmade collages always look better. I like it to be obvious that the work is a piece of collage and that you understand how the image was created. I have nothing against working digitally, though – most of the time at *Businessweek* I end up doing everything in Photoshop because there are always last-minute changes and we are working around the clock to send the magazine to the printer in time.

From where do you tend to source your images?
For the collage work I do at *Businessweek*, they all come from stock photo websites like Getty Images or Alamy. For the music posters and other works, sometimes they're just random stuff I have at my house or desk that I try to do something with before throwing away.

Have you ever used anything unusual in a collage?
Not really, but I have cut up important documents or books by mistake and ended up using them because … well, mainly to make myself feel better for the fact that I ruined something.

POSTER FOR BURNT ONES VS CREEPING CREEPING PINK + HÄXXAN
at Little League Shows. Digital collage, 2015

Little League Shows Presents: BURNT ONES —————— (Garage/Psych, US)

Mon, 16.11.   CREEPING PINK ———— (LoFi, US)
Doors 7pm, Show starts 8pm
                                       HÄXXAN ———— (Garage Punk, Tel Aviv)
Schokoladen
Ackerstr. 169   Aftershow: Dj Frank Freshness   (punkfunksoulr'n'r)

POSTER FOR USELESS EATERS at Little League Shows. Digital collage, 2015

CAMERON SEARCY

Originally from Knoxville, Tennessee, Cameron Searcy is a graphic designer who lives and works in Seattle, Washington. His commercial work has seen him create pieces for large brands such as Starbucks and Coca-Cola alongside other more independent musical acts and venues. Using a combination of digital and handmade techniques, Searcy both appropriates existing images and objects and uses his own photographs to create collages that embrace variety in colour and form.

POSTER FOR SILVERSUN PICKUPS at The Masonic Lodge at Hollywood Forever. Digital collage, 2015

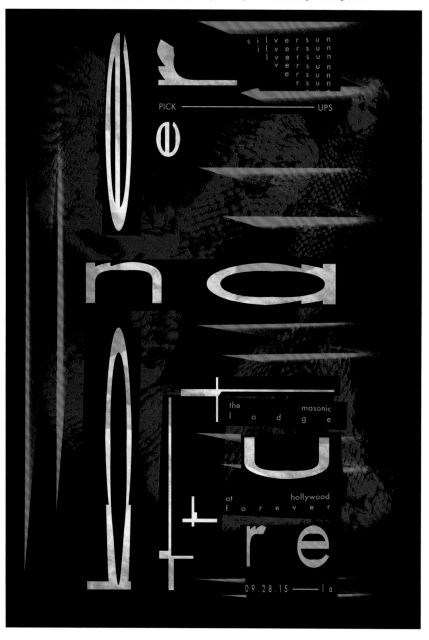

Opposite: POSTER FOR MSSINGNO.
Digital collage, 2015

VILLAGE UndeRground
55 holywell Ln
London uk
JOHNSON VOLCANO
with om b y →m u mean ce → special-
Nov 10
10 PM
2015

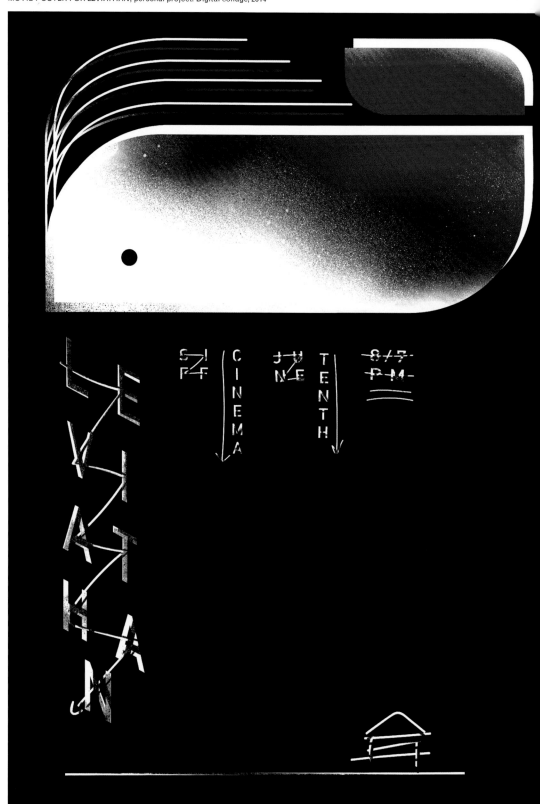

When did you first come across collage?
When I first started out, I hadn't gone to a school for design, so I had little to no intentional exposure to that sort of thing. I think I first started interacting with collage when I realized I couldn't draw for shit in design school but also that I was decent at composition and needed to get projects done. So sometimes collage is kind of a crutch, but I think it also gives the work its own character. It's a way of drawing and seeing in its own right.

What else attracts you to the medium of collage?
There's something inherently lo-fi about the whole process and there are very few rules about how it should or shouldn't be done. In a kind of perverse way I think it's one of the more honest processes; it's very upfront about borrowing good ideas from surprising places and then recontextualizing them to create something new. I would say it's analogous to mixing a fantastic album or song – you abstract or amplify what might go unnoticed in other works or recordings to create a focal point in a new piece.

From where do you tend to source your images?
Everywhere, really – the Internet, shitty photos taken from my phone, weird scans of objects I find in the office where I work ... sometimes they are very well-known pieces of artwork pulled straight from Google that are then highly abstracted.

Do you prefer to make collages digitally or by hand?
I've done it both ways, but lately I've been working digitally more, if only because it helps me work faster. When I decide to produce or print something, I'll usually go back and apply some analogue techniques where I had previously been using digital stand-ins. I also enjoy faking things, though: creating analogue effects through digital means.

Have you ever used anything unusual in a collage?
A photo of my own hairy nipple, which isn't so weird I guess – it's a pretty standard dude nipple as nipples go.

Do you have a favourite piece of design that uses collage?
The album artwork for the booklet and cover of Sufjan Stevens's *The BQE* is some of the most emotive stuff I've seen in a very long time. I love it – and the album sounds as good as it looks which always helps. I would also say the recent Future Islands album cover for *Singles* [see page 34] is very apropos and well executed.

Z-AXIS FILM FESTIVAL POSTER,
personal project. Digital collage, 2014

POSTER FOR BING & RUTH at SubCulture Arts Underground. Digital collage, 2015

Opposite: POSTER FOR DJEMBA DJEMBA
at Decibel Festival. Digital collage, 2014

DAMIEN TRAN

Damien Tran is a graphic designer and printmaker who works and lives in Berlin. He is the co-founder, along with Marion Jdanoff, of Palefroi, a micro-publishing company producing limited editions of artists' books, screen-printed zines and art prints.

Tran's use of collage is perfectly balanced in its technical approach. Each precise element is arranged with the overall intention of creating a piece that feels simultaneously systematic in method and wonderfully surreal in appearance.

POSTER FOR OPA, BLACK HEINO AT WEST GERMANY. Hand-cut collage and screen print, 2013

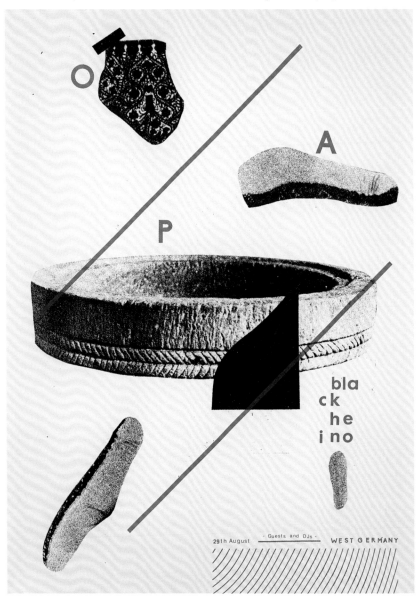

Opposite: POSTER FOR DAAU at Into the Great Wide Open festival. Hand-cut collage and screen print, 2013

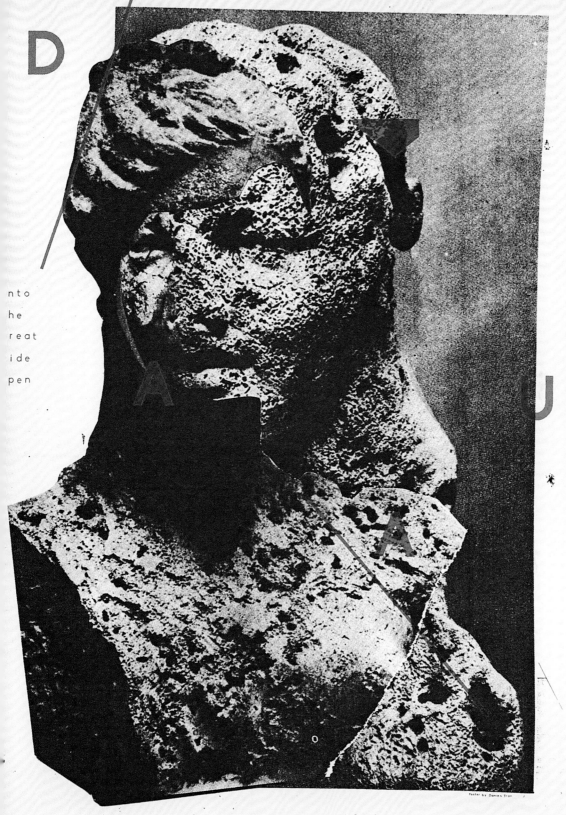

D

nto
he
reat
ide
pen

A

U

A

Poster by Damien Tran

7, 8, 9 September 2013

POSTER FOR WHITE FENCE. Hand-cut collage and screen print, 2015

Why did you first start making collages?
I came to collage because I was too lazy to learn how to draw.

And why do you think you have stuck with it?
I like the unpredictable aspect of this medium. Very often, you start with a clear idea in mind and it transforms into something completely different. Also, collage is a great way to collaborate with others, even if collage isn't an artist's main, usual practice.

Do you ever use any particularly unusual methods?
This isn't really unusual but I sometimes screen-print on top of collaged pieces. I like the cohabitation of flat and solid inks with different kinds of paper.

From where do you tend to source your original images?
At the beginning I used a lot of materials from old books and magazines. But with time I got tired of using vintage photographs and recognizable figures. I found that I was more interested in textures, so now I tend to only use imagery that I produce myself, which includes Xerox textures, drawings, patterns, cut-out paper, etc ...

Do you prefer to make collages digitally or by hand?
I like imperfect and unfinished things. Computers are great tools, but they give me too much temptation to control, correct and edit everything until it is clean and perfect.

Who is your favourite collage-based artist or designer?
I love the work of a duo called Strawdogs from Groningen in the Netherlands. Their collages are really colourful, abstract and weird. They mostly use their collage work as source material for their screen-printed gig posters.

POSTER FOR TEAM BUILDING.
Hand-cut collage and screen print, 2014

Opposite: POSTER FOR FLATSTOCK at Reeperbahn.
Hand-cut collage and screen print, 2014

DAMIEN TRAN

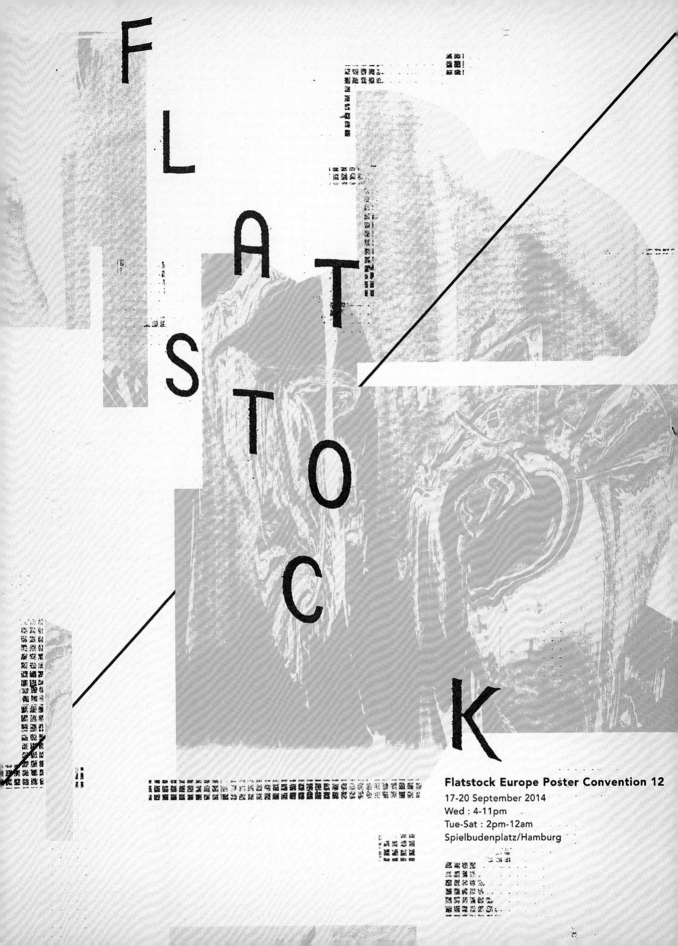

FLATSTOCK

Flatstock Europe Poster Convention 12
17-20 September 2014
Wed : 4-11pm
Tue-Sat : 2pm-12am
Spielbudenplatz/Hamburg

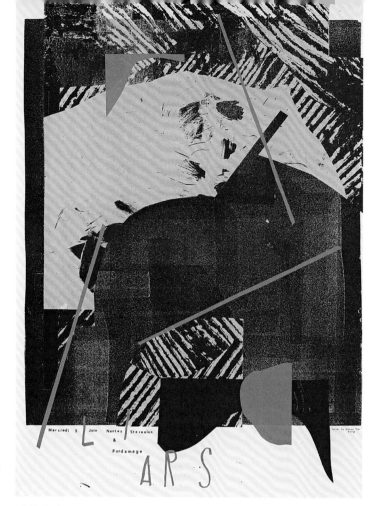

POSTER FOR LIARS + FORDAMAGE at Stereolux, Nantes.
Hand-cut collage and screen print, 2013

EXHIBITION POSTER FOR 'QUIET VIOLENCE'.
Hand-cut collage and screen print, 2014

POSTER FOR SCREEN-PRINTING WORKSHOP AT REPLICA, a graphic design and screen-print studio. Hand-cut collage and screen print, 2013

DR.ME

We are a Manchester-based creative studio under the name of DR.ME (which stands for our individual names, Ryan Doyle and Mark Edwards). We create record sleeves for labels including Tri Angle, Young Turks and Memphis Industries, and poster art for The xx, MIDI Festival and YoungArts Miami. In 2015 our studio launched its '365 Days of Collage' project (see pages 64 and 65), for which we spent a year creating a collage a day. It was inspired by our stay at the home of the collage artist Paolo Giardi, whose work covered the walls from floor to ceiling. This sparked a conversation about the speed of collage-making, which then led to the suggestion of creating a different piece every day for a year. The collage work that we typically create is focused around the use of perspective, juxtaposition and pattern, resulting in pieces that are at times psychedelic, surreal and disturbing.

POSTER FOR MIDI FESTIVAL (photography Jonathan Flanders). Handmade collage, 2014

VINYL SINGLE COVER FOR 'CONNECTED' by D/R/U/G/S (Moshi Moshi Records). Handmade collage, 2011

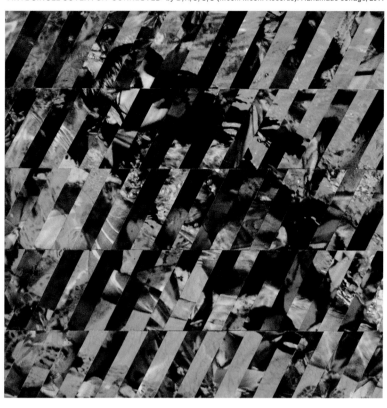

CLOUDWATER BREW CO LABEL. Handmade collage, 2015

When did you first come across collage?
[DR – Ryan Doyle]: My mum used to give me a photomontage of myself each year for my birthday.
[ME – Mark Edwards]: My mum, Jilly Edwards, is an artist, so it was probably watching her create collages in her sketchpad when I was a kid.

Why do you think your attraction to collage has endured?
DR: It's the unexpected nature of it. You can have a clear idea in your head about what you want to create, but when you actually start the process, everything changes. I enjoy the journey from start to finish: the mistakes, the 'eureka' moments and the happy accidents. I don't think a collage ever looks how you intended it to appear from the start. Which is a good thing.
ME: Similarly, it's the element of surprise, especially when making collages by hand. Despite the fact that you're mostly just using paper and glue, that moment when you put one thing next to another has the ability to transport you to a different universe – you get this incredible, strange and unexpected rush.

From where do you tend to source your imagery?
DR: From anywhere and everywhere, really. I tend to stay away from Google, though – too much choice is a bad thing when it comes to collage; I like the constraints of not having everything at your fingertips. More recently I have been trying to avoid *National Geographic*, purely because it seems to be everybody's go-to collage archive and you can sometimes see images begin to cross over into other people's work. I frequently find that using original or friends' photography always has the most rewarding outcome.
ME: Everywhere, really. Whenever I go to a different city I try to go to a charity or thrift store and pick something up. It could be anything from a local sports journal to a family album.

Have you ever used anything unusual in a collage?
DR: Personally no, but I did see a poster by a recent Glasgow School Of Art graduate who used spaghetti, which I thought was really cool. I guess anything could be part a collage when you think about it.
ME: Probably blood on a couple of occasions, but never on purpose.

Do you prefer to make collages digitally or by hand?
DR: By hand as much as possible, although there have been times when I have searched on the Internet for material to fill in the missing elements of a piece. Even then, though, I still print off and cut out the image so that it has the tactile quality that I look for in a collage. I am a traditionalist in that sense. There are too many options when working on a computer; I like limitations and only working with what you have to hand.
ME: I also prefer to make collages by hand. It forces you to make clear decisions from the outset on what it is that you're making. On a computer you can spend days doing, undoing and then redoing a certain piece but if you're sticking something or cutting something out by hand you have to be decisive.

Do you have a favourite piece of design that uses collage?
DR: Probably all the collage work by Dash Snow. I remember when I first saw it and I was just blown away – I felt an instant connection with it, and I think it sparked my interest in collage as a medium. His Saddam Hussein/New York collages are just wild and definitely worth checking out.
ME: I really love *Toshi Wa Sawayakana Asa Wo Mukaeru* (*The City Welcomes a Fresh Morning*) by the artist Tsunehisa Kimura [see page 7]. It shows New York being washed away by a waterfall and was later used on the album sleeve for *Zonoscope* by Cut Copy.

SINGLE COVER FOR 'WHO ARE YOU?' by Spring King
(Highs & Lows/PIAS). Handmade collage, 2015

SINGLE COVER FOR 'DUGA-3' by Evian Christ (Tri Angle). Handmade and digital collage, 2013

BOOK COVER FOR *BURDENS BY WATER* by Alan Rifkin
(Brown Paper Press). Handmade collage, 2015

ELLERY
JAMES
ROBERTS

Between 2008 and 2012, Ellery James Roberts's visual style became synonymous with his artwork for the Manchester-based band WU LYF, in which he also sang and played the organ. Since then, though, Roberts has gone on to create solo music videos, albums and more.

His work often brings together visual representations of heaven and hell in perfect symbiosis that can both distress and – in equal measure – calm the viewer. Bleak office buildings seemingly tumble into each other while fires rage and other horrors occur. His work is both futuristic in style and feels connected to the past with its use of analogue photography.

ALBUM COVER FOR *GO TELL FIRE TO THE MOUNTAIN* by WU LYF (LYF Recordings). Handmade collage, 2011

PLAY HEAVY POP POSTER for WU LYF. Handmade collage, 2010

What first sparked your interest in the medium of collage?
As a kid, I used to keep a scrapbook of cut-outs taken mostly from the weekend newspapers. It was, in effect, a 2-D toy that enabled me to go to any world that the newspapers gave me access to. I became interested in collage as an actual practice a little later, though, when I discovered the *détournement* works made by the Situationist International.

Why do you think your attraction to collage has lasted?
I enjoy the mindful act of cutting with a razor-sharp blade; I'm not as interested in the finished piece as I am about the process of cutting up and collecting imagery. In fact, I consider my best collages to be the temporary compositions on the walls or floors of wherever I am living or working. I think all the pieces that have been published in this book were made specifically to illustrate ideas for my old band WU LYF – pretty graphics to accompany pretty sounds.

From where do you tend to source your images?
The Internet. I used to spend hours searching through second-hand junk, as if a found image was more real for its chance discovery rather than the instantaneous ease of a search engine. It's super romantic, right – I call bullshit on this nostalgia fetishism now. My understanding is that there is mutual ownership of all content created by the human species. The individual is a node to the masses – every photo, every piece of creation is a contribution to our collective experience. Collage is perhaps the most basic way to go about continuing this collective experience, but, at its best, collage finds something truly new in the juxtaposition of old ideas.

Do you have a favourite piece of collage?
I recently came across some collages by Thomas Hirschhorn. Brutal balances of spectacle and the real, they feel pretty sexy and are relevant to the way we consume imagery today.

ELLERY JAMES ROBERTS

BOOKLET ARTWORK FOR 'SUCH A SAD PUPPY DOG' from the album
Go Tell Fire to the Mountain by WU LYF (LYF Recordings). Handmade collage, 2011

ELLERY JAMES ROBERTS

WU LYF POSTER, accompaniment to the album *Go Tell Fire To The Mountain*
(LYF Recordings). Double-sided, Risograph-printed and handmade collage, 2012

IS AN ARTIST LED COOPERATIVE
OF 2010. THE LYF WAS FORMED
BETWEEN ... IN SEARCH
... DATE THE LYF
... SIVE OF PETTY
... LITERATURE
... VESSEL THRU WHICH TO
... INDIVIDUALS,
... NAL PARTIES.
... NOT BOUND
... OTHER. THE LYF IS
... SUFFICIENCY;
... OF MONETARY
... SEARCH OF AN
... ONLY TO AN
... AND AVOID FORMS OF
... DISMANTLE.
... THE POWER
... LABORATORS
... CURIOSITY ABOUT
... INK IT OUT.
... AGENT FOR
... GATEKEEPER
... N'T NEED TO
... UR OWN BIG
... CALLING HAVING TRUE FUN.

HISHAM AKIRA BHAROOCHA

Hisham Akira Bharoocha is a Japanese-born artist currently based in Brooklyn, New York, and is signed up to the Hugo & Marie agency. After studying at Rhode Island School of Design in the mid-1990s, he has since created work for clients including Puma, Facebook, Sony, *Nylon Magazine*, *Die Zeit Magazine*, Nowness and marketing company Oglivy & Mather.

Bharoocha's collages are enthralling melting pots and juxtapositions of incongruent images – from a baby thrush diving out of the mouth of an old woman (see below) to the splicing of the head of a snake with the face of a woman (see page 75). The dream-like, surreal manner of his artworks is enhanced by the combination of different media and materials, which include hand-cut paper, found imagery and spray-painted shapes.

BIRD CALL. Ink and collage on paper, 2009

THE BACK AND FORTH. Acrylic paint on hand-dyed canvas, 2012

LVSESF. Collage on paper, 2014

Talk me through your approach to creating collages.
I love creating something from found images because of the feeling
I get when I come across something uncanny: an image that you would
not be able to conceive of prior to seeing it. I like recontextualizing
images, shapes and objects to create an abstract narrative or a surreal
vision, like something in a dream or a nightmare. People's minds are
wired in all different ways, and relationships between them and objects,
shapes, forms, people, animals and so on differ from person to person.
I like making images that make you think about how all of our minds are
wired differently, or at least make you wonder what inspired a person
to make an image like the one you are looking at.

Whose collages particularly inspire you?
Some of Yamatsuka Eye's record cover work for his band Boredoms
was a huge inspiration to me whilst growing up. I also remember seeing
Tadanori Yokoo's poster artwork as a kid: paper collages that were then
silkscreened afterwards. His design work is incredible – to this day
I find myself looking at these images time and time again. I couldn't
possibly single out just one piece by either of these artists as I love
so much of their work. Later on I discovered the work of Dieter Roth,
which I was very much inspired by.

Do you recall your first exposure to collage as an art form?
I remember going to see an Outsider Art exhibition as a teenager,
where I saw the work of Henry Darger, who used collage in a different
way by bringing together his drawings and paintings. My mom then
turned me onto 'Kirie', the Japanese art of paper cutting.

Do you prefer making collages digitally or by hand?
I prefer making collages by hand for my fine art work and digitally
for commercial work. I used to do my commercial work by hand and
making revisions was a nightmare. I would often need to create a whole
new piece of work because a client didn't like one element that I had
inserted. Working digitally, you have so much more flexibility. With
my fine art pieces, I like having a limitation to the number of materials
at hand.

Do these limitations mean that you have been forced to include some
particularly unusual materials?
I try to use as many unusual things in my collages as possible. I often
use backgrounds of photographic advertisements from the 1970s or 80s
as you sometimes find these amazing, soft, airbrushed gradations from
one colour to another.

Usually, though, from where do you source your images?
Mostly vintage books that I find at a low price, but I also like mixing
in materials from high-gloss magazines to combine different textures.
The way books were printed in the past is incredible. I have a love/hate
relationship with cutting up books.

74

HISHAM AKIRA BHAROOCHA

HORT

Hort is a Berlin-based graphic design studio made up of a small group of creatives. Since its formation in 1994, Hort has become a pioneer in terms of reinventing the visual language of contemporary graphic design.

The collages created by Hort are always led first and foremost by experimentation. Although the studio does not have a signature aesthetic, adhering instead to a philosophy that revolves around individualism, Hort's collages are mostly handmade, giving a recognizably tactile quality to the finished images. There is also an emphasis on understanding fully both what the final image represents and the context behind each original component.

Hort's experimental enthusiasm has inspired many budding young designers, and consequently the studio has become a highly influential source of inspiration for its contemporaries. Its work has also been featured in countless publications, including *Creative Review*, *Printed Pages*, *Intern Magazine* and *IdN Magazine*.

RECORD SLEEVE FRONT AND BACK FOR *MEMENTO: ALBUM REMIXES 2* by Booka Shade (Get Physical Music). Handmade collage, 2005

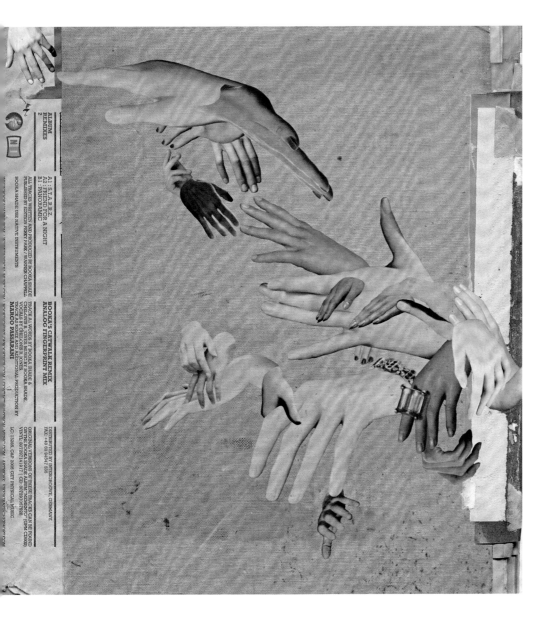

RECORD SLEEVE INNER GATEFOLD FOR *MEMENTO: ALBUM REMIXES 2* by Booka Shade (Get Physical Music). Handmade collage, 2005

Do you have a preference for any specific piece of collage?
  [Eike König, Founder and Creative Director of Hort]: Not one special one,
  but I would encourage people to take a look at work by artists such as
  Max Ernst, Hannah Höch and Alexander Rodchenko, among many others.

From where do you tend to source your materials?
  From the Internet, magazines and the flea market.

Why do you think you keep returning to the medium of collage?
  It's the idea or concept behind collage that always draws me to it.
  Collage is very versatile: it can be used in all kinds of disciplines
  like film, literature, architecture, sculpture, etc.

"one love to give
            one life to live
nothing to find
            we're just wasting time"

VISUAL CAMPAIGN FOR ALLUDE CASHMERE.
Handmade collage, 2011

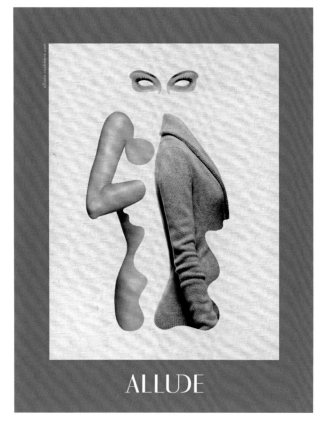

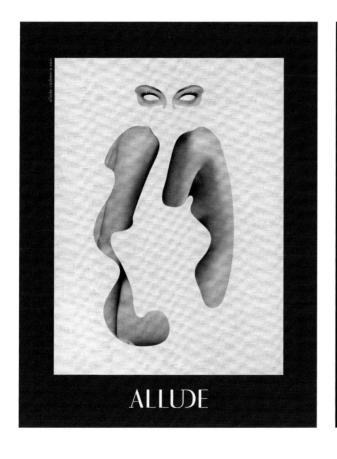

HVASS&
HANNIBAL

Comprising two creatives by the names of Nan Na Hvass and Sofie Hannibal, Hvass&Hannibal is a design studio based in Copenhagen. Since opening in 2006, the pair's work has evolved but has also maintained a dreamlike infatuation with colour and form. The studio has worked extensively with the band Efterklang across various formats, from record sleeve designs (see below) to stage sets for a series of shows at the Sydney Opera House.

Another name on the stellar list of creatives signed up to the agency Hugo & Marie, Hvass&Hannibal's output is uncynical, starry-eyed and almost childlike in its craft-based approach. Surreal and ethereal landscapes are often conjured up (see pages 82 and 87), inspired by the studio's interest in folklore.

ALBUM COVER FOR *PIRAMIDA* by Efterklang (4AD). Digital collage, 2012

EFTERKLANG
piramida

Opposite: THE POWER OF TWO, editorial illustration for *Viewpoint* magazine issue #33. Digital collage, 2013

What attracts you to the medium of collage?
 [Nan Na Hvass, co-founder of Hvass&Hannibal]: The possibility
 of creating interesting visual combinations – for example, combining
 geometric imagery with a photograph of a mountainscape.

Do you have a favourite individual collage?
 We have an Inka Järvinen collage on our wall that we love.

Do you use found or ready-made materials or do you make them
from scratch?
 Mostly we make our material ourselves, but sometimes we use Sofie's
 father's landscape photography.

Have you ever used anything particularly unusual in a collage?
 Hmmm, I don't think so ... but many years ago Sofie made a penis-
 shaped collage made out of images of flowers.

DRAWN TOGETHER, wrapping paper for *Wrap* magazine issue #7. Digital collage, 2013

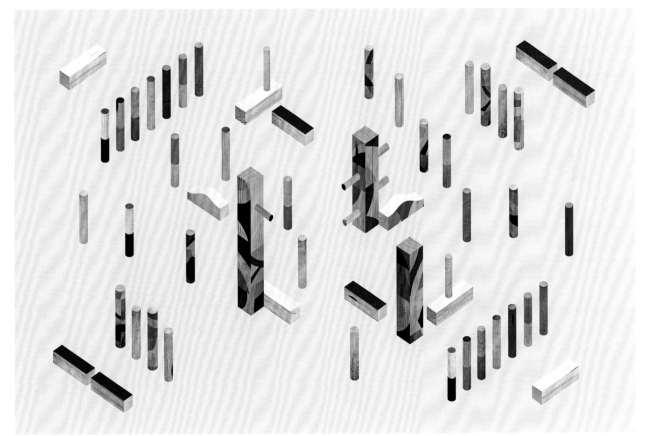

MONKI, editorial illustration for *Monki Magazine*. Digital collage, 2013

INGE
JACOBSEN

Inge Jacobsen was born in Galway, Ireland, and raised in Denmark. After graduating from Kingston University, London, in Fine Art Photography in 2011, she has since worked as a professional artist. Working mainly with found commercial imagery, she uses embroidery as a way of physically intervening whilst not losing the original message of the image.

Her use of embroidery in conjunction with contemporary commercial images is her way of connecting traditional, largely feminine, interests from the past with the present day. It is also her way of reclaiming the female form through the use of traditional female craftsmanship (largely seen in her pornographic illustrations).

Jacobsen's work has been exhibited around the world. In 2012 she was invited to exhibit her pieces alongside Sarah Lucas's as part of SHOWstudio Shop's *Selling Sex* show. In 2011 the luxury brand Georg Jensen invited Jacobsen to re-energize their Spring/Summer 2012 campaign. Her more recent clients include American Express, Le Bon Marché and Parisian fan-makers Duvelleroy.

UNTITLED, editorial illustration for *TANK Magazine*. Woven paper, 2014

When did you first come across collage?
I first came across collage at school, in art class. I thought it was great – you could manipulate ready-made images and drop them into completely different contexts.

Where do you find your ready-made images now?
I tend to source my images from fashion magazines such as *Vogue*, *Vs. Magazine*, *Love Magazine*, *i-D*, etc. I prefer to use contemporary commercial images – often designer ad campaigns – as a way of appropriating the original commercial message behind the image.

Do you ever use any unusual materials?
The most unusual thing I've ever used in a collage is thread. I use a lot of thread in my art and it is often mixed in with newspaper, magazine pages or photographs.

Do you prefer to make collages digitally or by hand?
All of my collages are made by hand. The process of cutting up the image and physically rearranging it really appeals to me. Most of my collages are woven pieces – either two copies of the same image woven together or two different images woven together. The process was inspired by the Danish 'Julehjerter' (pleated Christmas hearts) we used to make as kids. For me, the physical act of creating the collages is the main appeal.

What other collage-based designs have inspired you?
Henri Matisse's *Cut-Outs* are some of my all-time favourite pieces. I am also a huge fan of John Baldessari's *Dot* series in which he placed coloured price stickers over movie stills and photographs.

UNTITLED, editorial illustration. Thread on paper, 2013

Opposite: UNTITLED, editorial illustration. Woven paper, 2014

LINDBERG CAMPAIGN. Woven paper, 2013

WOVEN VS MAGAZINE, editorial illustration. Woven paper, 2013

JELLE
MARTENS

Jelle Martens is a visual artist living and working in Ghent, Belgium. His collages typically juxtapose images of the environment with formal elements of design, although these formal, geometric elements are always subordinate to the content. There is a general ambiguity to his images, which increases the scope for plural meanings and multiple visual expressions.

Martens divides his time between designing album covers, working on commissions from various cultural centres and focusing on personal projects. Whether his work is commissioned or self-initiated, he favours a personal approach as a starting point for creating his images.

VERVAL (DECAY), personal project. Digital collage, 2014

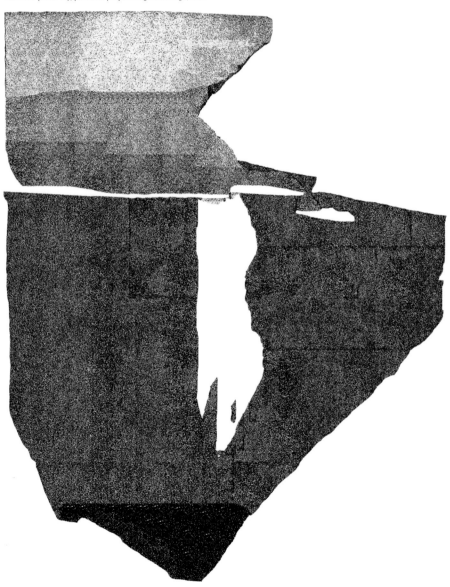

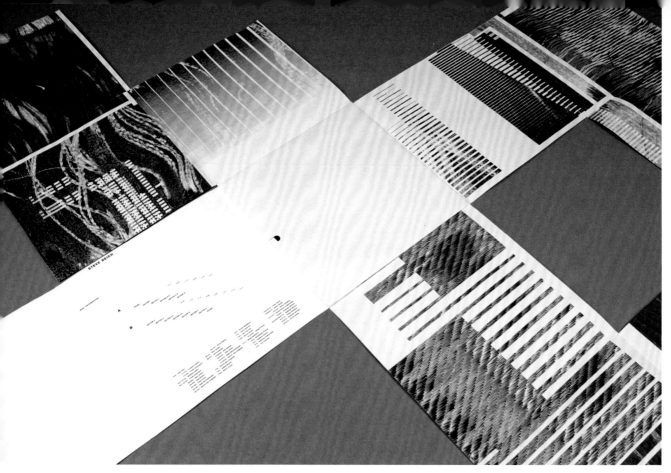

:II:, record sleeve (from box collection) based on *Music for 18 Musicians* by Steve Reich, personal project. Handmade and digital collage, 2013

Do you have a favourite design that uses collage?
Collage with Squares Arranged According to the Laws of Chance by Jean Arp. For me this is a work that goes back to the definition of collage. Arp fixes on the most important aspects – form, colour and composition – giving each element the right amount of devotion. As a result, the work is timeless. Ellsworth Kelly's collages also fascinate me. By combining abstract shapes and images of recognizable objects, such as news articles or buildings, these objects are also rendered purely aesthetic.

From where do you tend to source your images?
There is no one, fixed source. I try to capture moments in an organic way, and these sources, or origins, can take on various meanings. They could be sounds, small accidents, an atmosphere I happen to find myself in, as well as formulated ideas. It is important to stay open-minded. I also try to avoid repetition, which is another reason why I don't rely on one particular source of inspiration. There are always inspiring sources, ideas and pathways that are yet to be discovered. I'm much more interested in making discoveries and challenges. For instance, the starting points for *Natuur* and *Motorcross* [see page 95] were the scrapbooks that belong to my father. They fascinated me in

terms of text, images, cover texture, colours, format, detail ... I felt the need to capture these different aspects and turn them into a collage.

Have you ever used anything unusual in a collage?
For my Master's thesis, I designed the packaging for a record collection that included compositions by Arvo Pärt, Steve Reich and William Basinski. I scanned small textile stickers – the ones you can put on the inside of clothing – and magnified these scans. The process of zooming in on one image revealed small, unseen details, which complemented Steve Reich's approach in his compositions.

Do you prefer to make collages digitally or by hand?
There is definitely reciprocity between both techniques. I often make collages by hand as part of my research, either sketching or cutting and pasting pieces together. It's a slow process, but it makes you more reflective and eliminates artifice. However, working digitally can lead to entirely new directions. Although working by hand offers me greater insight, I find it hard to work exclusively with one technique. Often it is the interaction between these techniques that creates a certain tension and intrigues me most of all.

JELLE MARTENS

COVER ARTWORK FOR 'STAND UP/SO FAR' by A.A.L. (AGAINST ALL LOGIC) (Other People). Digital collage, 2014

VERVAL (DECAY), personal project. Handmade and digital collage, 2010

VERVAL (DECAY), personal project. Handmade and digital collage, 2014

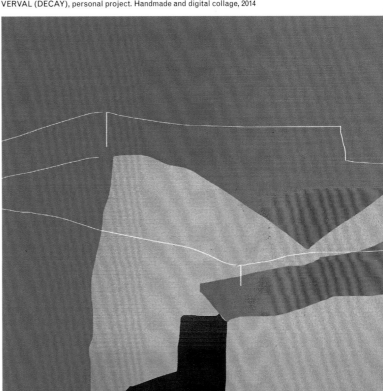

JESSE DRAXLER

A Minneapolis-based artist, Jesse Draxler's creations are dark and sinister, with a Frankenstein-like fusion of found imagery, typography and design sensibilities. His aesthetic is both moody and visually bombarding, which is achieved largely through the combination of bold imagery and a monochrome colour palette. Often Draxler covers sections of his images with solid black shapes (see page 103, bottom), leaving the viewer to wonder what lies beneath. His very distinctive style has courted clients that range from revered publications, such as *The New York Times*, to bands Deafheaven and The Black Queen and even SOVRN Skateboards company.

ILLUSTRATION FOR *THE NEW YORK TIMES*. Digital collage, 2015

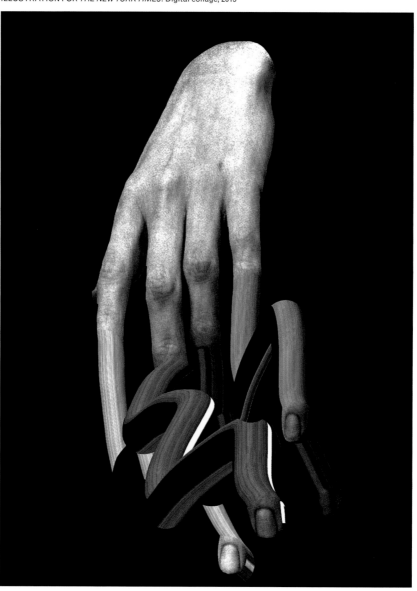

Opposite: UNTITLED, personal project. Handmade collage, 2015

UNTITLED, personal project. Handmade collage, 2015

UNTITLED, personal project. Handmade collage, 2015

ILLUSTRATION FOR *THE NEW YORK TIMES*. Digital collage, 2015

JESSE DRAXLER

From where do you tend to source your imagery?
For a lot of my material, I work with a photographer. I provide a concept for the image beforehand and then act as an art director on set. I still source found imagery as well, though.

Do you prefer to make collages digitally or by hand?
It's all about balance – I like to do both.

When did you first come across collage?
I once wrote a thesis on the assimilation of subculture aesthetics into the mainstream and used punk as a case study. I think that was when I first started experimenting with the medium.

And what do you think its initial appeal was?
Its immediacy.

Finally, have you ever used anything unusual in a collage?
No, I'm not into kitsch.

UNTITLED, personal project. Handmade collage, 2015

SINGLE COVER FOR 'FROM THE KETTLE ONTO THE COIL'
by Deafheaven (Williams Street). Digital collage, 2014

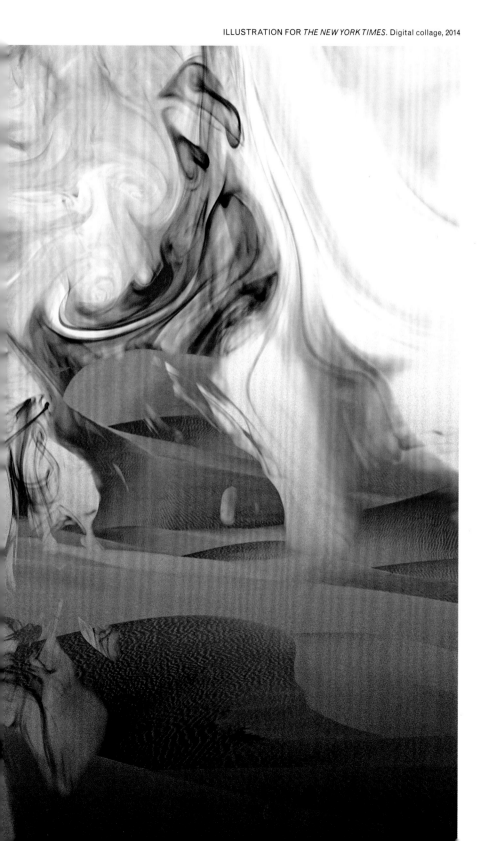

JOEL
EVEY

Based in New York and Philadelphia, Joel Evey began his graphic design career at Pixar, which was instrumental in developing his individual, animated style with its appearance of a 3-D world on a 2-D page. Although Evey then left Pixar to design Urban Outfitters's catalogues, hang tags and posters, there is a feeling of movement and a tangibility to almost all of his subsequent works. Notable for also having worked with *Bloomberg Businessweek*, Levi's and Nike, Evey uses type in a particularly nonchalant and stylish way. He has also introduced bright colours into his more recent work, whereas before his palette was mostly monochrome.

COMMANDMENT, personal project. Digital collage, 2015

Opposite: UNTITLED, personal project. Digital collage, 2015
Overleaf: JAMROCK for Urban Outfitters. Digital collage, 2015

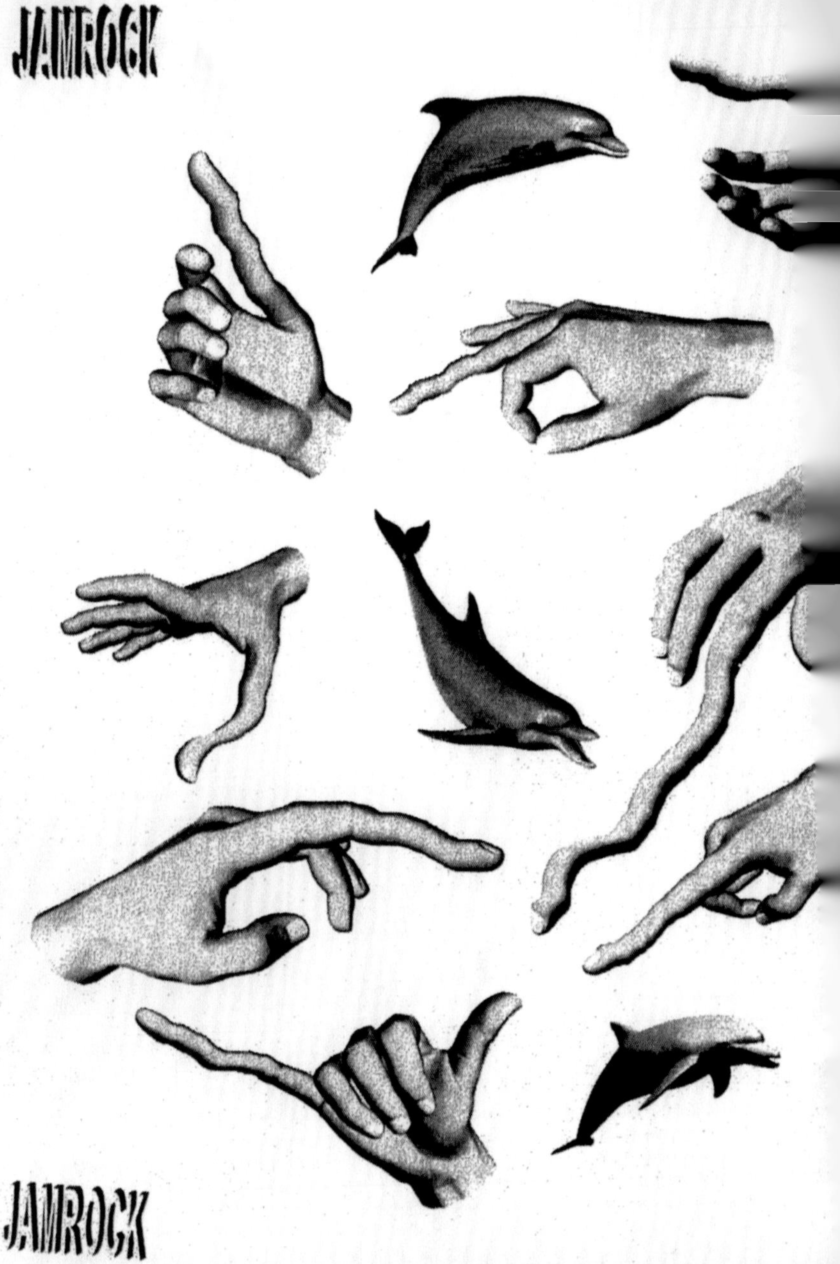
JAMROCK
JAMROCK

JOEL, self-promotional project. Digital collage, 2015

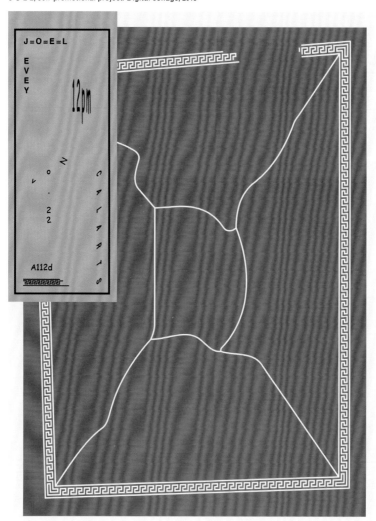

Why do you enjoy making collages?
I enjoy the ability to create multi-layered images and also to change
both the form and meaning of a single image. You can create any
narrative you want with collage.

Do you prefer working digitally or by hand?
I like making collages digitally. There are so many more possibilities
when working within a digital space.

Do you tend to source your images digitally as well?
I find my images everywhere. Mostly I take them from the Internet,
but also from magazines, old books, bits of photos, etc.

What's the most unusual thing you've used in a collage?
Duct tape and grape jelly.

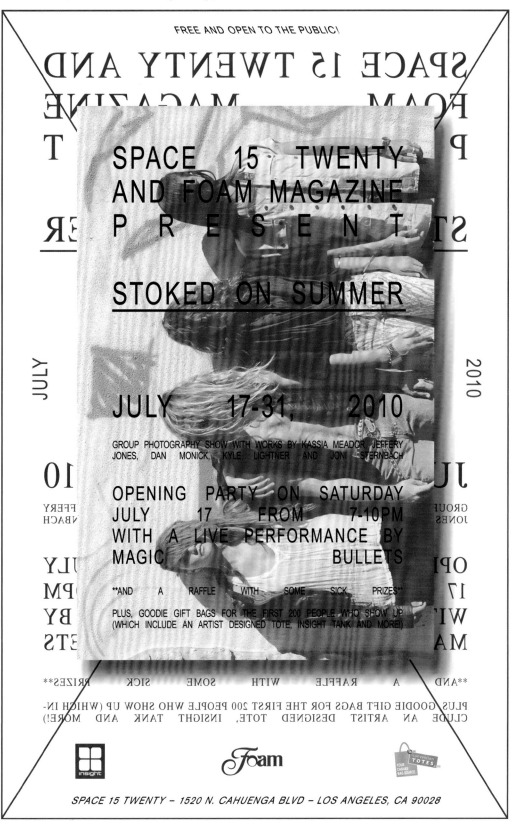

FREE AND OPEN TO THE PUBLIC!

SPACE 15 TWENTY
AND FOAM MAGAZINE
P R E S E N T

STOKED ON SUMMER

JULY   17-31,   2010

GROUP PHOTOGRAPHY SHOW WITH WORKS BY KASSIA MEADOR, JEFFERY
JONES, DAN MONICK, KYLE LIGHTNER AND JONI STERNBACH

OPENING   PARTY   ON   SATURDAY
JULY   17   FROM   7-10PM
WITH   A   LIVE   PERFORMANCE   BY
MAGIC   BULLETS

AND   A   RAFFLE   WITH   SOME   SICK   PRIZES

PLUS, GOODIE GIFT BAGS FOR THE FIRST 200 PEOPLE WHO SHOW UP
(WHICH INCLUDE AN ARTIST DESIGNED TOTE, INSIGHT TANK AND MORE!)

SPACE 15 TWENTY – 1520 N. CAHUENGA BLVD – LOS ANGELES, CA 90028

JOHN POWELL-JONES

John Powell-Jones is a Manchester-based illustrator, printer and educator, whose previous projects include making record sleeves for Moon Duo and Opal Tapes record company, as well as posters for bands Mogwai and Demdike Stare. Regardless of whether he is screen-printing, monoprinting or using a Risograph printer, Powell-Jones's pieces always possess his signature playful style and look as though they were composed instinctively. His love of horror movies, graphic novels and experimental and left-field music are all clearly visible within his work for both clients and his personal projects.

ALBUM COVER FOR *LET GO* by Xosar (Black Opal). Digital collage using handprinted elements, 2015

XOSAR

POSTER FOR SACRED TAPES PRESENTS. Digital collage using handprinted elements, 2015

JOHN POWELL-JONES

From where do you tend to source your imagery?
I spend a lot of time in print rooms collecting and filing any scraps of paper I find. Practising traditional print processes tends to produce a lot of misprints and mistakes, which can be momentarily frustrating. However, they can also provide great resources for future image-making.

Do you prefer to make collages by hand, or do you ever work digitally?
I much prefer to keep away from the computer for as long as possible. Working by hand, I feel like I'm more open to chance, whereas it's too easy to 'undo' things when working digitally. Also, I often find myself restricted by the size of the screen, and I always get a headache if I look at it for too long.

Do you remember the first collage that particularly inspired you?
The first work that I recall having a real impact on me was John Heartfield's *Adolf the Superman Swallows Gold and Spouts Tin*, which I first saw when I was at college. (Although I think that's probably a photomontage rather than collage.)

Which artists have influenced you the most since then?
Corita Kent has been a big influence on my practice. I very much enjoy the way she turns the everyday and mundane into things of beauty, especially with regards to her approach to colour and typography. I also love Damien Tran's work [see page 54]. His show posters for Micachu and the Shapes, Liars and King Khan immediately spring to mind, but all of his work is pretty great.

Do you ever use any particularly unusual materials?
I've only been using collage as a way of producing commercial work for the past couple of years, so it's still a fairly new medium for me and I've yet to become very adventurous. I have been building up a lot of my material by using a Risograph to scan 3-D objects, which has produced some interesting outcomes, although I haven't found the right project yet to put this practice to good use.

POSTER FOR *SHADOW OF THE SUN* ALBUM LAUNCH. Handmade collage, 2015

114

Opposite: FROM 'AT REST', a series of images commissioned by Demdike Stare. Digital collage and screen print, 2015

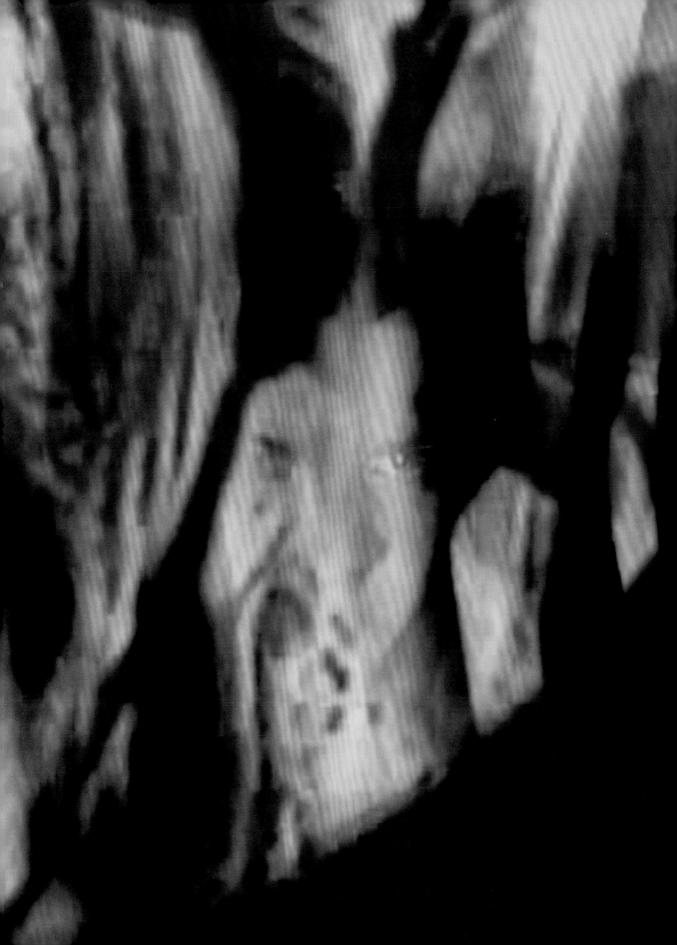

JULES
JULIEN

Born in France, Jules Julien now lives and works in Amsterdam after studying Applied Arts there. From his 'Black History Month' work for Nike to his unique record sleeve design for Lorde (see below), Julien's style succeeds in being simultaneously dark and winsome. Preferring to work digitally rather than using handmade techniques, his collages are dark and introspective, often exploring the divide between fantasy and reality. Common motifs in his work include human faces, skin, body parts and clothing, which, in turn, betrays Julien's preoccupations with eroticism, death and identity.

LIMITED-EDITION SINGLE COVER FOR 'TEAM' by Lorde, for the Secret 7" project. Digital collage, 2015

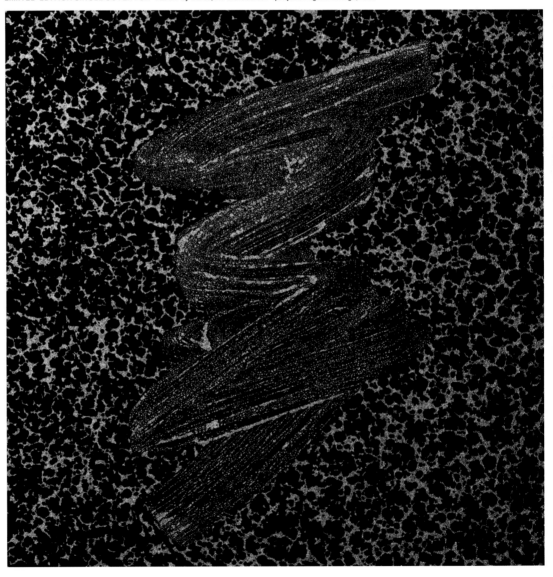

Opposite: EMPEREUR, personal project. Digital collage, 2015

When did you first start making collages?
I began making collages when I was fifteen years old and a student. I think my first one was a decoration of my school portfolio using photos of fashion models and some Peter Beard images, all taken from a magazine. It ended up being a mixture of body parts and photos of Africa and dead animals.

Why do you think you are drawn to the medium of collage?
The startling impact of the images; the accidents that often reap the best results; the collision of different universes that would never ordinarily meet.

Could you give some examples of how you create these juxtapositions in your images?
I use a wide range of images and materials, trying to make them cohabit. To give a few examples: a cat and a gun; human bodies and Nasa views of space; typography and soapy water.

Do you prefer to work digitally or by hand?
I much prefer doing digital collages. I use digital tools to draw shapes out of different sources and then 'stick' them together.

Where do you go to source your images?
I look everywhere, but the first place that I go to is my enormous stock of fashion magazines, which I have been buying since I was a teenager and which I absolutely treasure.

Whose collages inspire you the most? Is there one specific piece of work that has stood out for you?
I have several favourites. I love the work of Daniele Buetti and his collage-based fashion pieces – they are particularly impressive. I also remember a collage-style Sex Pistols poster called *Who Killed Bambi* by Jamie Reid that I fell in love with when I was a teenager.

FROM 'BLACKOUT', a series of print-based installations for RISE Berlin art gallery. Digital collage, 2013

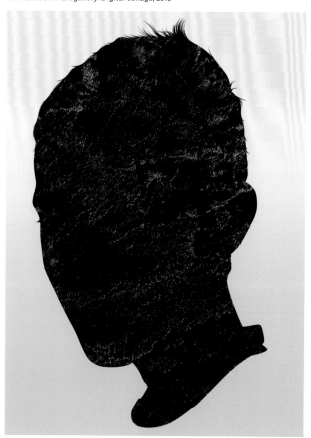

KUSTAA SAKSI

Finnish-born illustrator Kustaa Saksi lives and works in Amsterdam, and is represented by the creative agency Hugo & Marie. He is well known for his abstract collage designs, which typically combine antiquated forms of art – for instance, Art Deco, Orientalism or Futurism – with a psychedelic folk aesthetic. His illustrations have been featured in numerous magazines and publications all over the world, and he has collaborated with brands including Nike, Swarovski, Sony PlayStation and Lacoste.

Specializing in graphic storytelling through pattern design, textile art and installation, Saksi builds fantastical worlds of playful and paradoxical shapes, environments and psychedelic atmospheres, all of which seem simultaneously troubling and inviting. His recent work makes extensive use of the Jacquard weaving process (see pages 123 and 124) and takes inspiration from the visual delusions induced by migraines and the state of sensory confusion that exists between sleep and wakefulness. Nature and the sea also strongly influence his pieces for the Marimekko home collection (see page 125).

PLAY SET FREE, brand poster for the 'This is For the Players' campaign celebrating PlayStation 4, commissioned by 180 Amsterdam. Digital collage, 2014

NIGHTLESS NIGHT, from the *Reveille* collection. Jacquard-woven tapestry made from mohair wool and rubber, 2014

Opposite: BLOOD BROTHERS, from the *Hypnopompic*
collection. Jacquard-woven tapestry made from mohair
wool, merino wool and acrylic, 2013
Overleaf: COVER OF *DEE MAGAZINE*. Digital collage
using hand-drawn elements, 2014

Describe your first experience of collage.
  When I was three years old, I very much liked making cut-and-
  paste pictures.

From where do you tend to source your images?
  I always draw the separate elements myself. I then like to compose
  my images by putting these elements together in the style of a collage.

What do you think is the appeal of collage?
  I think it's the unexpectedness of the process. You can create something
  wholly different and original out of very familiar elements.

What is the most unusual collage-based piece you have created?
  I think my series of tapestry installations, entitled *Hypnopompic*,
  kind of work as three-dimensional collages.

MARIMEKKO PRINT, from the *2015 Homeware* collection.
Produced as fabric, home textiles and tableware. Digital collage, 2015

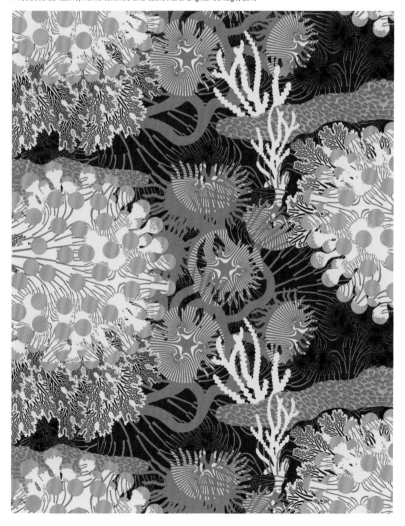

LEE
NOBLE

Originally from Nashville, Tennessee, Lee Noble is a creative living and working in Los Angeles. His projects span the media of art, design, music and craft, and he has spent time in New York under the tutelage of illustrator Mike Perry (see page 192).

Noble's work is highly influenced by his use of Risograph-printing and screen-printing, embracing their restrictions in colour and tone to create pieces that are wonderfully muted. He tends to make record sleeves, cassette tape covers and posters for clients, as well as working on his self-initiated projects, such as making artwork for his own record label, No Kings Records.

ALBUM COVER FOR *RUINER* by Lee Noble (Bathetic Records). Risograph print. Handmade collage on paper, 2013

Opposite: CONSTRUCTION. Risograph print. Handmade collage and chalk on paper, 2013

When did you first come across collage?
I can't pinpoint the precise moment. I remember that once in grade school there was an assignment to make a collage on the theme of 'What America Means to You'. I covered this huge posterboard, and I vaguely recall the teacher leaning over and telling me mine was the best! I can't say what it looked like, but I think a large part of it involved pictures of aliens. In high school my friends and I really loved Barbara Kruger and we had photocopies of *When I Hear the Word Culture I Take Out My Checkbook* in our lockers.

What would you say is now your favourite collage?
Off the top of my head ... *Almanac* by Robert Rauschenberg.

What attracts you to the medium of collage?
Simplicity of technique, an egalitarian attitude and depthless complexity of meaning and composition.

Do you prefer to make collages digitally or by hand?
By hand, although I often print out low-quality images from online sources or from phone pictures, etc., and blow them up. I just love the immediacy of physically cutting and arranging, with no glowing screen.

From where do you tend to source your images?
Mostly old books and magazines grabbed from yard sales and bins. I love 1970s editions of *Popular Mechanics*, books about science and nature, and yearbooks. Sometimes I just find shapes and I don't even properly look at what they are – they could be anything as long as they work aesthetically.

Have you ever used anything unusual in a collage?
I use a lot of photocopied, scanned or Risographed plant matter, e.g. leaves or petals, to get the right textures or patterns.

ALBUM SLEEVE FOR *MEETS GRUESOME*
by Poet Named Revolver (No Kings Record Co).
Risograph print. Pencil and gouache on paper, 2014

J-CARD FOR *SUNLESS* by Coupler (No Kings Record Co). Letterpress and Risograph-printed collage on cardstock, 2013

PINK FLAG, poster. Risograph print on Neenah sundance paper, 2015

J-CARD FOR *SECRET HANDSHAKE* by Sigbrand (No Kings Record Co). Risograph-printed collage on paper, 2015

J-CARD FOR *SUNLESS* by Coupler (No Kings Record Co). Letterpress and Risograph-printed collage on cardstock, 2013

LEE NOBLE

J-CARD FOR *PLAYS THE HITS* by Dan Svizeny (No Kings Record Co). Risograph-printed collage on paper, 2013

J-CARD FOR *MEDITERRANEAN YEARS* by Tim Coster (No Kings Record Co).
Letterpress and Risograph-printed collage on paper, 2012

LEIF PODHAJSKÝ

Australian graphic designer Leif Podhajský creates work that is consistently Daliesque, whether it is advertising images for giant conglomerates (Nike and Bose), posters and album artwork for major recording artists (Kelis, Tame Impala, Grimes and Shabazz Palaces – see following pages) or cassette tapes for independent musicians. Amongst the psychedelic patterns, swathes of bleached-out kaleidoscopic landscapes and hypnotic mirror effects, the juxtaposition of incongruent images enhances his Surrealist aesthetic. There is also an intriguing contradiction between his evidential appreciation for nature and his digital manipulation of imagery.

SINGLE COVER FOR 'RUNNING ROMEO' by Gypsy and The Cat (Sony Music). Digital collage, 2010

LEIF PODHAJSKÝ

Do you prefer to make collages digitally or by hand?
I much prefer working digitally. I love to make mistakes, and working digitally enables me to do so. But I still do work manually from time to time ...

From where do you find your source material?
Anywhere and everywhere – the Internet, copies of *National Geographic*, old books, photographs.

Of all the materials you've used previously, is there one that particularly stands out?
I once used a photo of a beautiful young Fulani tribe girl from Bida, Nigeria, for the artwork for a Shabazz Palaces record. I got permission from the photographer but he wasn't so keen once I'd collaged her face. I explained that I was trying to express the surreal aspects of the music ... I guess I can see where he was coming from.

What attracts you to the medium of collage?
Two things seen or placed close together with contrasting effect. Juxtapositions are a very interesting way to explore initial concepts.

Do you have a favourite piece of design or illustration that uses collage?
Anything Hisham Akira Bharoocha [see page 72] does – he has such a smooth style, plus he's a rad guy. We once had a joint exhibition together in Melbourne and we got to hang out.

GRIMES POSTER for 'The Mythical Gymnastics Tour'. Digital collage, 2012

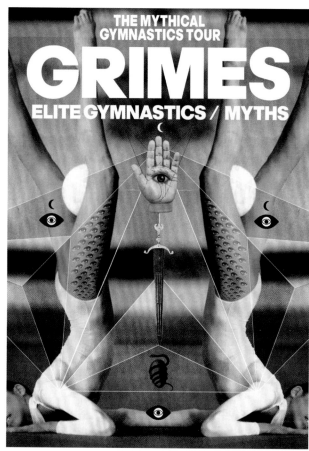

FOLLOW, used for Tame Impala T-shirt print. Digital collage, 2011

ALBUM COVER FOR *LIVE @ KEXP* BY Shabazz Palaces (Sub Pop). Digital collage, 2012

ALBUM COVER FOR *THE NORTH BORDERS*
by Bonobo (Ninja Tune). Digital collage, 2013

ALBUM COVER FOR *DREAM CAVE* by Cloud Control
(Ivy League Records). Digital collage, 2013

FIBONACCI VORTEX, art print. Digital collage, 2014

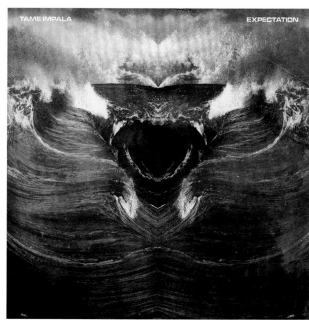

SINGLE COVER FOR 'EXPECTATION' by Tame Impala
(Modular Records). Digital collage, 2010

ALBUM COVER FOR *INNERSPEAKER* by Tame Impala (Modular Recordings). Digital collage, 2010

LEIF PODHAJSKÝ

LEWIS MCLEAN

Originally from Milton Keynes in the UK, Lewis McLean is currently based in Manchester where he creates work predominantly for record labels, experimental music events and independent music venues. His clients include Tombed Visions Records, Islington Mill in Salford, Soup Kitchen in Manchester and Fat Out, also based in Salford.

In his artwork for clients working within the music business, McLean typically combines a Surrealist collage of images – for instance, a skeleton attempting to skewer a fly resting on a planet (see page 143) – with sans-serif fonts. Two disparate worlds – text and image – collide and fuse as one.

POSTER FOR PLANK. Digital collage, 2014

PLANK.
&Vei

www.facebook.com/Plankuk
www.planknation.bandcamp.com

thebayhorsepub.co.uk

The Bay Horse
35-37 Thomas Street
Northern Quarter

CASSETTE SLEEVE FOR *SECRET PATHS* by I Have Eaten the City (Tombed Visions). Handmade collage, 2014

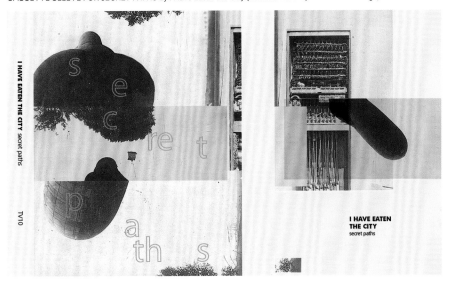

CASSETTE SLEEVE FOR *I DIDN'T MIND YOU IMPROVISING, I JUST WISH YOU'D DONE IT BETTER*
by Andreae/Birchall/Cheetham (Tombed Visions). Handmade collage, 2014

BOHRENNOIR, art print. Digital collage, 2015

What first inspired you to make collages?
I can't remember exactly when I first saw a collage – I might've stumbled across some Dadaism in my youth. However, I can recall when I was first really inspired to make a collage. I was studying graphic design at Shillington College and stumbled across Mark Weaver's work for Bēhance. It was a project called 'Make something cool everyday'. I was instantly amazed at the sort of imagery he used in his work; the composition and typography were so clean. His is still the benchmark I am trying to reach … but the guy is just too good.

Do you prefer making collages digitally or by hand?
I try to practise both ways as much as possible, but the majority of the work for clients ends up being digital, especially when having to design things according to certain dimensions, such as CDs, vinyl records, posters and cassette tapes. Using a program like Photoshop makes it so much easier to get the work complete and to the size and specifications that the client desires. I know there are purists out there that dismiss collages if they are done digitally and I can see their point. The ease of using software like Photoshop takes away the restrictions of collaging by hand. If I'm making a collage purely as a form of artistic expression, I always try to make it by hand. But as a graphic designer I will try and answer the brief by any means.

Do you think there is an inherent tension between freedom and restriction in collage?
It's this restricted freedom that I enjoy both as a practising artist and as a viewer. I revel in having a handful of images that I then try to reconstruct to form a new message or put them in a new context, like a jigsaw puzzle. Working that way really stimulates me, and it is also really inspiring to see how others respond to those restrictions and witness what they produce. I was never particularly good at drawing, so creating collages was a way for me to express myself. When I first came across the medium I identified with it straightaway: it was a style I believed I could achieve and that anyone else could achieve if they wanted to. I think that's why I love it so much and continue to practise it.

CASSETTE SLEEVE FOR *WREN / LE CHAT EST PARTI* by Joseph Quimby JR (Tombed Visions). Handmade collage, 2014

Opposite: COMIC DEAD, personal project. Digital collage, 2015

From where do you tend to source your images?
  When I can, I source my images from the old bookshops in Manchester.
  Most of the time I have something specific in mind when I visit, and if
  I can't find the physical image, I will have a look on public domain sites ...
  places like Flickr, Google, Tumblr, etc. This is usually the way I work when
  I have a brief that demands something specific from me. I am sure I'm
  like most collage artists in that I am constantly on the lookout for new
  images to source. They can reveal themselves anywhere at any time,
  so you always have your eyes peeled.

Your typography often adds another dimension to the finished piece.
Are typographical style and placement things you consider even when
creating the initial collage of images?
  Yes, a lot of the work I do is gig posters or artwork for bands, so
  typography is a big feature in the design. I used to just create a collage
  and then try and squeeze the type in where I could. Looking back at
  some of my old work, I find it shocking that I had the audacity to do
  this – some of the posters were really bad! Now I always consider the
  composition of the images and typography as one rather than either
  being an afterthought. Typography is so important in design and as soon
  as I started appreciating it on the same level as the images, I think my
  work instantly started to improve.

THE SHOWER ACT, personal project. Handmade collage, 2015

LINDA
LINKO

Linda Linko studied at Aalto University of Art and Design in Helsinki. In 2010 she set up her own studio there, working as a graphic artist and illustrator, and she has since become known mostly for her posters and collage art.

Linko's remarkably simple compositions usually consist of cut-out or torn coloured card that has been collaged together, with hand-painted or hand-drawn typography written on top. Everything is achieved by hand, which results in an effortless, joyful and carefree style.

Linko's numerous clients include the Red Bull Music Academy, Frame Publishers, *Wallpaper* and *ELLE*. In 2014 she was also asked to exhibit her work alongside other creative luminaries at Pick Me Up, a graphic arts festival at Somerset House in London.

FRAME #100, illustration for the 100th issue of *Frame Magazine*. Hand-cut collage, 2014

Opposite: POSTER FOR DAPHNI at Red Bull Music Academy.
Hand-cut collage and ink, 2014

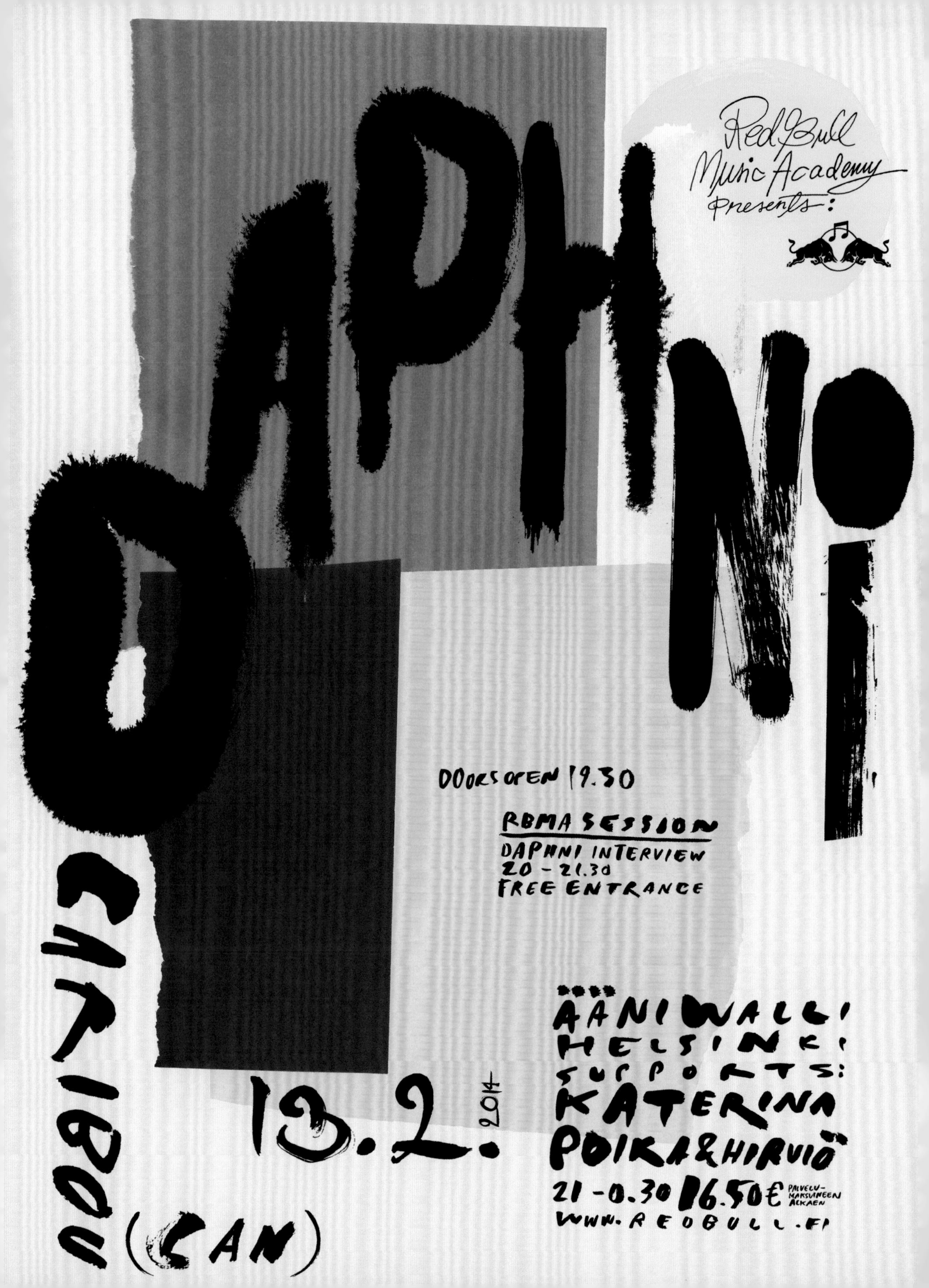
DAPHNI
Red Bull Music Academy presents:
DOORS OPEN 19.30
RBMA SESSION
DAPHNI INTERVIEW
20 - 21.30
FREE ENTRANCE
ÄÄNIWALLI
HELSINKI
SUPPORTS:
KATERINA
POIKA&HIRVIÖ
21 - 0.30
16.50€
PALVELU-MAKSUINEEN ALKAEN
WWW.REDBULL.FI
13.2.
2014
CARIBOU (CAN)

When did you first come across collage?
Like most people, in art class at primary school. Later on, at university,
I started making collages again, trying out different things in my
sketchbooks. Back then I didn't think that my practice would amount
to anything, and it was a shame that I quit making my sketchbook
collages when I started working. However, I rediscovered my old style
a few years ago when I was challenged to come out of my comfort zone
in a design project. At the time my work was mainly black and white,
but suddenly I was forced to use colour. Making these bright and vivid
collages felt far more natural than the black-and-white paintings and
drawings I was doing then.

Why do you think your attraction to collage has endured?
The process is similar to the challenge of solving a puzzle. I typically
choose one piece and go from there, and it's so rewarding when you
find seemingly odd pieces that go together. I also love playing with
colours. I paint and draw only in black and white, so I guess my colourful
collages offer a pleasing contrast.

What kind of materials do you typically use in your collages?
Photography, paper cut-outs, ink paintings, drawings – all kinds of
materials. The right piece could be basically anything, from the rubbish
that happens to be on my table to the rug beneath my feet. I mainly
look at the colour and texture. Mostly I am inspired by my photography.
I love to go through my holiday snaps and, for example, choose a piece
of sandy beach or a mountain, and start from there. And as I draw and
paint a lot, I frequently use those as materials as well.

Do you prefer to make your collages digitally or by hand?
I try to make all my work by hand, but often I find that digital formats
give your collage more depth. By that I mean it is easy to enlarge or
scale down images according to what is needed for the overall effect.

Have you ever used anything unusual in a collage?
I don't really think there *can* be anything unusual in a collage. I often
choose images that mean something special to me, or include a piece
of myself in a way so that no one can see it. Once I used a close-up
photograph of a dessert that my friend made for me by putting it into
a club poster.

149

Left: FRAME #100, cover for the 100th issue
of *Frame Magazine*. Hand-cut collage, 2014
Right: PANAM, fine art print. Mixed collage, 2014

SALVADOR. Hand-cut collage, 2014

GUATE. Hand-cut collage, 2014

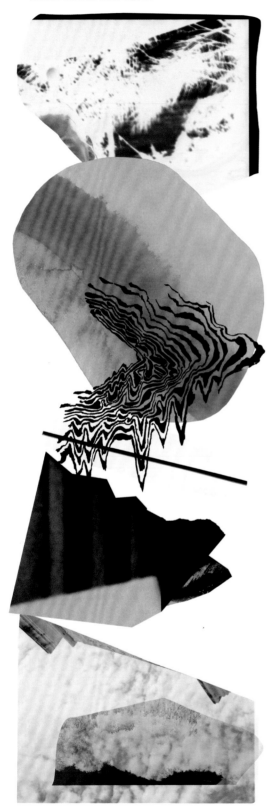

LINDA LINKO

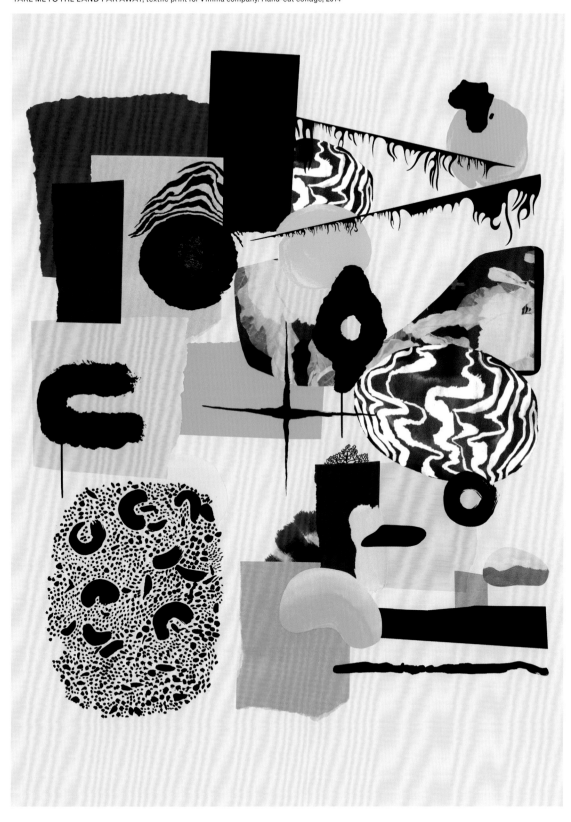

LOUIS REITH

Louis Reith lives and works in Amsterdam. After studying graphic design and working at an advertising agency in Antwerp, Belgium, he moved back to the Netherlands to study Art and Crossmedia Design at the Academie voor Kunst en Industrie (AKI) where he received his BA in 2010. During this period Reith started exploring and experimenting with abstraction. As well as his personal projects, he has since created artwork for albums by Half Way Station and Nick Storring, among others.

With a fascination for typography and book design, while trying to avoid the computer as much as possible, Reith's first project was a series of abstract ink drawings. Using a combination of bold graphic shapes found within books and old maps, he created a world of mountainous landscapes and sculptures where the ultra-graphic competed with the natural.

In his more recent body of work, Reith delves deeper into his reflection on the boundaries between graphic design, fine art and nature. Working within a range of media, environments are disrupted by inert and obscure shapes. Whether reimagining black-and-white photographs as geometric landscapes, translating graphic elements into wood installations or painting with soil, Reith continually appropriates found objects and materials.

UNTITLED II, personal project. Handmade collage of book interiors, 2015

UNTITLED (NACHTTUIN 1), personal project. Collage of found book pages, 2014

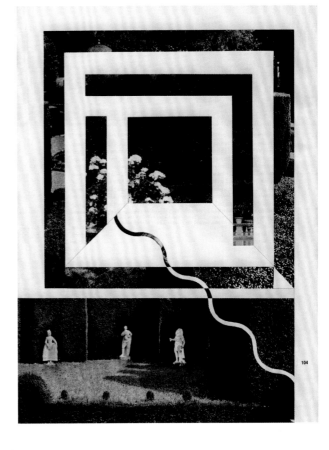

UNTITLED XI, personal project. Collage of found book pages, 2012

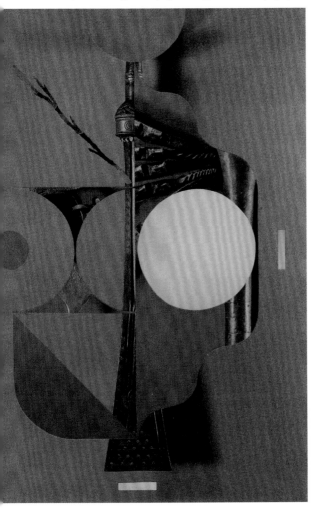

ALBUM COVER FOR *DODO* by Half Way Station (self-released). Collage of found book pages, 2015

ALBUM COVER FOR *GARDENS* by Nick Storring (Scissor Tail Records). Collage of found book pages, 2014

Do you have a favourite piece of design that uses collage?
I'm not necessarily interested in collage art. For inspiration I tend to look at work within other fields, such as installation art, painting and sculpture. Graphic design also plays a big role in my work.

Why do you think collage has become your medium of choice?
I think it has a lot to do with my interest in printed matter, specifically book design and layout. Out of all the different media with which I work, collage has the closest relation to my background as a graphic designer.

Do you prefer making collages digitally or by hand?
My practice of making collages actually arose from my aversion towards the computer. When I started studying graphic design, the whole industry was focused on the digitization of the world while I was more attracted to handmade objects. I truly believe that real magic happens when you can't completely control the outcome.

From where do you tend to source your images?
For my collages I mostly collect books that use a particular kind of paper or printing method that interests me or that I'm looking for specifically. Besides that, I'm very interested in natural and archaeological themes combined with monochrome photography. Black-and-white pictures of greenery fascinate me.

Have you ever used anything unusual in a collage?
Lately a lot of my works outside of collage have featured wooden pieces covered in soil. I would love to apply soil to my collages in the near future.

UNTITLED (NACHTTUIN 7A), personal project. Collage of found book pages, 2014

UNTITLED (NACHTTUIN 7B), personal project. Collage of found book pages, 2014

LOUIS REITH

MARIO
HUGO

Mario Hugo, a New York-based illustrator, designer and creative director, runs the hugely successful creative agency Hugo & Marie, which he founded in 2008 with his wife Jennifer Marie Gonzalez. Since then his clients have included Rihanna, Beck, *Flaunt Magazine*, Stella McCartney, Dolce & Gabbana, Lorde and Phillip Lim.

Hugo's personal work juxtaposes handmade textures with computer-generated shapes to create pieces that are both futuristic and nostalgic about tactile things. In terms of his artistic process, Hugo often buys old books, tearing out the images he wants or extracting and taping together the blank pages to form a canvas. Geometric shapes, drawn portraits, letterforms and other minimalist motifs then form additional layers, often applied with the use of China ink, graphite, gouache or acrylic in a distinctly muted colour range.

BRAND AND GARMENT ARTWORK FOR UNITED BAMBOO. Digital collage, 2011

ALBUM COVER FOR *YEAR IN THE KINGDOM* by J. Tillman (Western Vinyl). Digital collage using hand-drawn elements, 2009

BRAND AND GARMENT ARTWORK FOR UNITED BAMBOO. Digital collage, 2011

Whose collage-based work do you particularly admire?
I really love a lot of collage work out there – everything from the old stuff by Man Ray and Joseph Cornell through to folks like Hisham Akira Bharoocha [see page 72].

When did you first come across collage?
When you think about it, collage is everywhere. I think every room, street and desktop is effectively a collage of decontextualized elements, semiotics and weird juxtapositions that tell rich stories.

From where do you tend to source your images?
I source symbols from all over the place. I particularly love visiting the Strand Bookstore near Union Square in New York, although I haven't been there in the last couple of years. I then prefer to work digitally to create the final collaged image.

Have you ever used anything unusual in a collage?
Sure. I think that one of the central features of collage is the unexpected combination of certain elements, though I should also say these elements are rarely random for me. The symbols that I include each have to have a home and a reasoning behind them, however abstract.

ALBUM COVER FOR *STRANGER* by Balmorhea (Western Vinyl). 3-D collage sculpture, 2012

ALBUM COVER FOR *THE CURSE OF SOFT ROCKS* by Soft Rocks (ESP Institute). Digital collage using hand-drawn elements, 2011

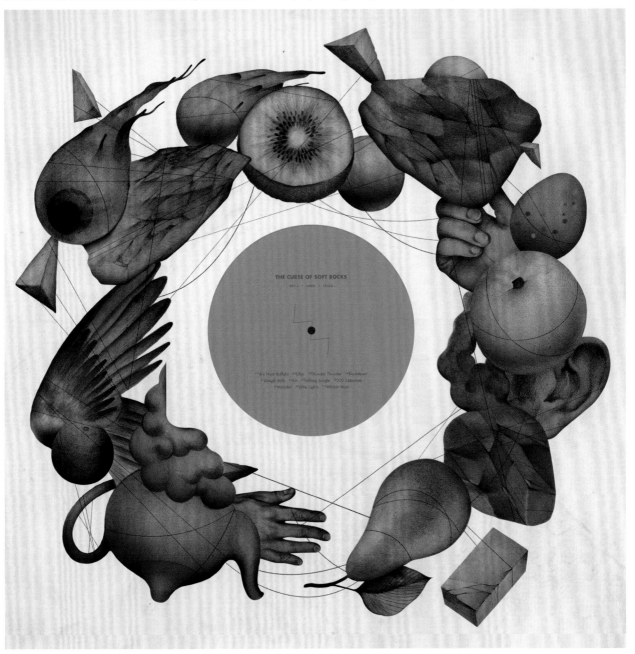

MAT MAITLAND

Mat Maitland is an image-maker, video artist and art director from St Albans in the UK. From a young age he became obsessed with music, fashion and magazines, which find their way very clearly into his work, and he has since created music campaigns for some remarkably big names: Michael Jackson, Prince, Elton John and Kylie Minogue. In recent years he has even taken his collage aesthetic into the realm of film, creating fashion videos for KENZO, Printemps Paris and Hunter Boots.

Maitland's collages are almost overwhelming in their glossiness and decadence – they are full of references to pop, fashion, vintage magazines, paintings and films. Although many of these references inspire nostalgia in the viewer, his aesthetic is also contemporary as a result of his Surrealist method: abstracting images and then placing them back together in a different context.

COVER FOR *THE ELEMENT YES* EP by Meanwhile (Fiction Records). Digital collage, 2014

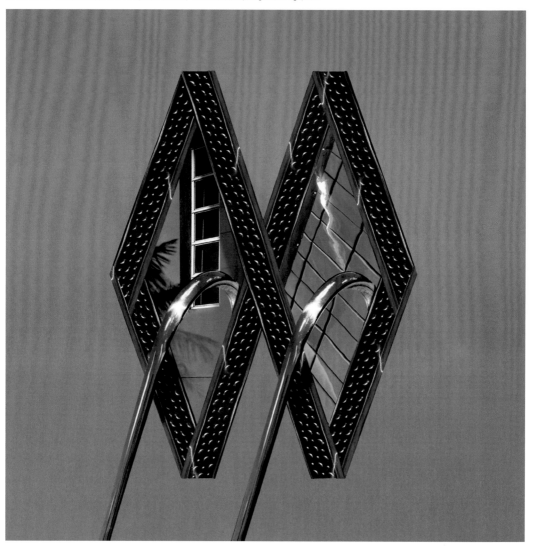

Opposite: MICHAEL JACKSON for *Clash Magazine*. Digital collage, 2014

ILLUSTRATION FOR *PLEASE!* MAGAZINE. Digital collage, 2014

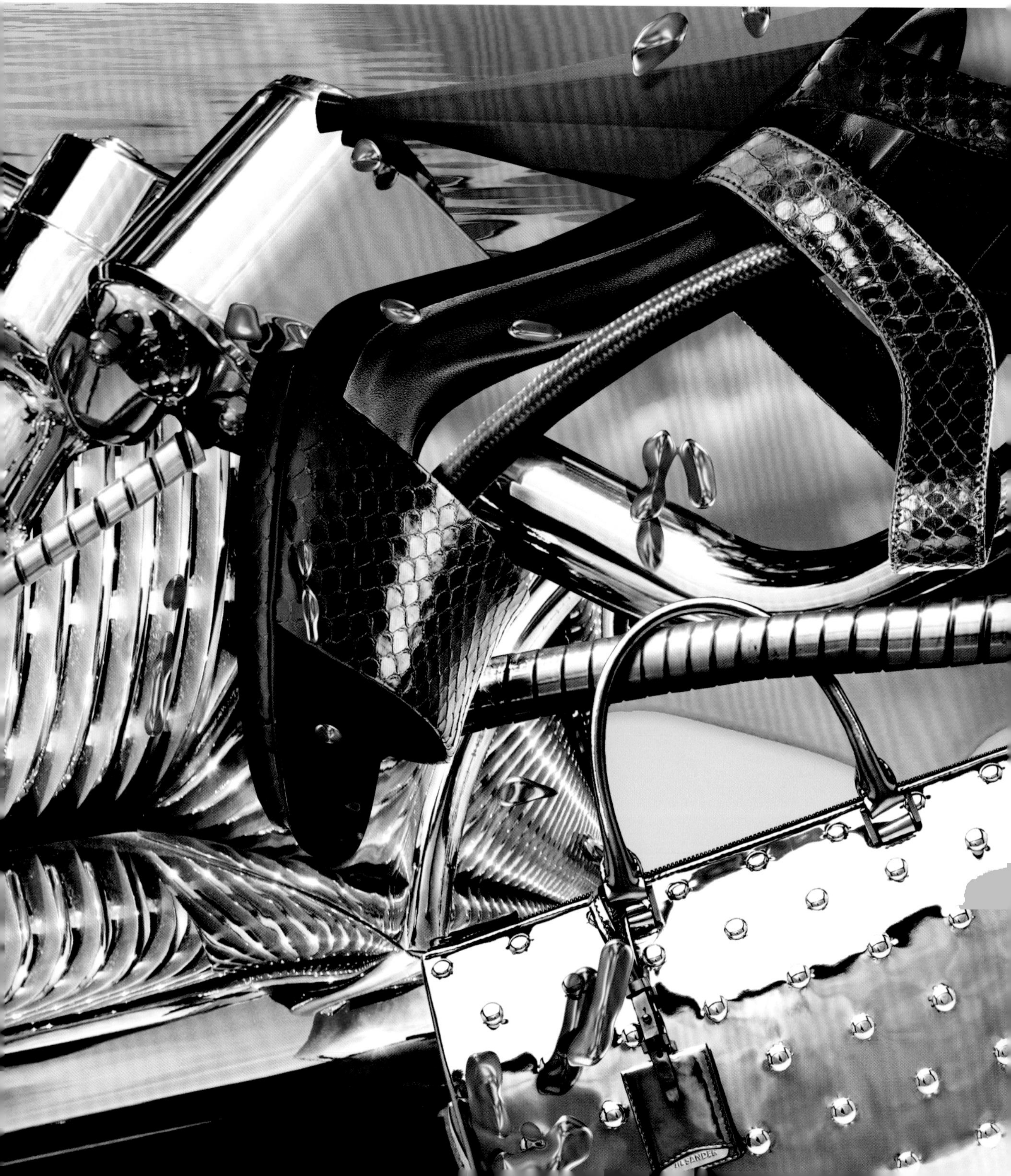

What was your first experience of collage?
  I was always doing collages at school and then at art school, either
  making my own record covers or keeping little collage sketchbooks (this
  time with good old-fashioned scissors and glue). But I wasn't really
  thinking of collage as a genre then; it was just a way of creating pictures
  with no boundaries.

Is it this lack of boundaries in collage that attracts you to the medium?
  Collage allows you to spin fantasies from the most mundane material
  that, in isolation, wouldn't amount to much. In a way, with collage the
  initial visual elements are a tool rather than an end point – they are the
  ingredients that make up the final image.

Do you prefer to make collages digitally or by hand?
  I make all my images digitally. This gives me the freedom to work on
  an image with speed and ease from a technical point of view, which
  then allows me to concentrate fully on the image itself from an artistic
  standpoint.

Have you ever used anything unusual in your collages?
  I often try and sneak my cat Quincy into my work. A few years ago I
  included him in a promotional video I did for fashion label KENZO
  (called 'Electric Jungle'). If you study it closely, you'll see him in there.

MATTHEW COOPER

Based in London, Matthew Cooper typically experiments with typography and strong graphic elements to create collages for clients ranging from esteemed publications (the *Financial Times* and *New Scientist*) to highly established bands, musicians and record labels (The Kills, Arctic Monkeys, Domino Recording Company). Cooper's style draws inspiration from the work of Kurt Schwitters and the other Constructivists who sought to replace the traditional concern with composition with a focus on construction. However, Cooper also uses more contemporary methods, extracting found material from books, magazines, records, CDs and assorted junk both ancient and modern.

ALBUM INNER SLEEVE FOR *SWIM* by Caribou (City Slang). Digital collage, 2010

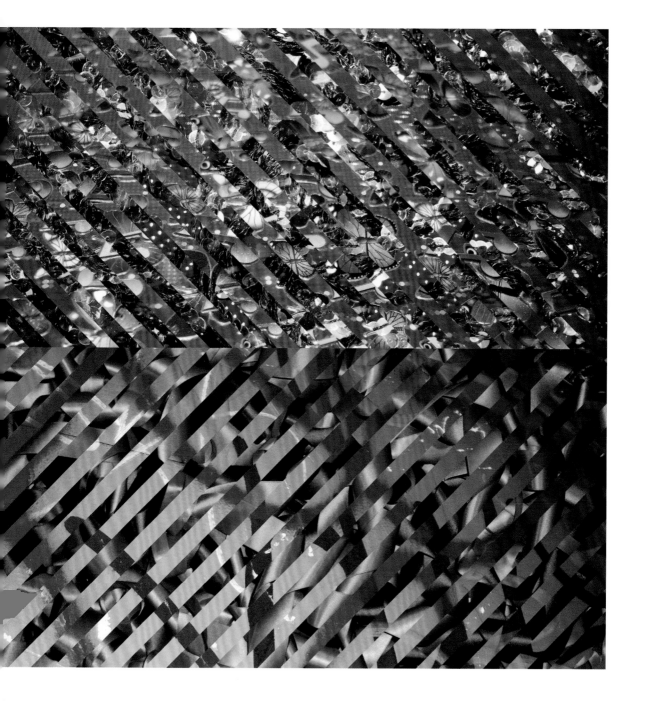

MATTHEW COOPER

When did you first come across collage? Since then, has one specific work emerged as your favourite?
I remember when I first saw the collages of Kurt Schwitters and Robert Rauschenberg – and I still often return to their work. The punk and DIY graphics of the late 1970s and early 1980s also left a deep impression on me, as did the *Work in Progress* record sleeve by Scritti Politti. In terms of my favourite, there are some paintings by Cy Twombly that I absolutely love, for example, *Pan* and *Bacchanalia-Fall (5 Days in November)*. His combination of mark-making and simple collaged elements is so exciting. I'm also a huge fan of the work of John Stezaker. His ideas are so simple but beautifully realized. He is much-imitated but, for me, he is the man!

What attracts you to collage?
I'm really drawn to the idea of juxtaposing images that aren't necessarily meant to be together in order to create something new and even construe the meaning of the original images.

From where do you tend to source your original imagery?
All over the place. I often source found imagery, but I also use my own photography and hand-painted and hand-drawn elements. I even used to use a lot of bleach. With the projects for Caribou and Four Tet [see following pages], I worked closely with the photographer Jason Evans, who supplied the raw photographic images.

Do you prefer to work digitally or by hand?
I like both, and I often incorporate handmade elements into my digital work. When working digitally, the trick is to try and retain the spontaneity and surprise of hand-created pieces without getting bogged down in endless tweaking. But tweaking can, of course, be useful!

EMISSIONS, for RMC Group. Digital collage, 2003

ALBUM COVER FOR *BEAUTIFUL REWIND* by Four Tet (Text Records). Digital collage, 2013

MATTHEW COOPER

CARIBOU

Swim

MATTHEW COOPER

MATTHEW CRAVEN

New York-based artist Matthew Craven creates collages on paper out of images from historical works of art and ink drawings. The collages are visually reminiscent of Dada photomontages, but they also work alongside more contemporary examples of images that appear on social media sites, such as Tumblr and Instagram. In his collages, Craven brings together images from multiple old history books, inviting both well-known and anonymous artistic voices from the past to engage in a transformative dialogue. He often then combines these images with detailed, hand-drawn lines or places them on an aged background – for example, vintage movie posters with yellowing tape. By placing the prehistoric next to the modern and compressing millennia, Craven interrogates the meaning of artistic legacy and influence, as well as the importance of cultural context to an artist's practice.

REVERSE, personal project. Found imagery and pen on paper, 2015

TOMB, personal project. Found imagery and pen on paper, 2015

DOUBLE, personal project. Found imagery and pen on paper, 2015

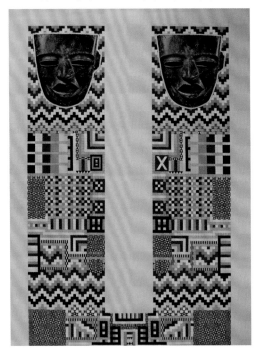

Did you make collages at the start of your artistic career or has this only been a recent development?
An assemblage by Ray Johnson inspired me to shift my focus from painting to mixed media. Whilst at grad school, I began making collages to avoid a painting I was working on. Those diversions got me my first show in New York, and now collage has become my full-time practice.

Why do you think your attraction to collage has stuck?
Despite the fact that it is a relatively new medium, only considered an art form in the last hundred years or so, I feel more connected to this practice than, say, painting or sculpture, which date back thousands of years.

From where do you tend to source your images?
All my pieces start with old history books. I use them to collage by hand (never duplicating, copying or reprinting images) or as inspiration to create new patterns. All of my work is then made on blank book pages or on the backs of old posters.

Do you prefer to make collages digitally or by hand?
Never digitally, always by hand. For me, digital art lacks soul. I also think it's more interesting to be doing analogue versions of Photoshop techniques in today's digital world.

Have you ever used anything unusual in a collage?
Not unusual, but I do occasionally like to sneak pieces of modern art into my collages.

Have you done many collaborative projects?
One of my favourite collaborations was with the musician Huerco S – I did the artwork for his album *Colonial Patterns* after it transpired that we were both interested in similar themes. With the musician Jordskred, I also released a cassette album called *Unseen Spaces* in 2014, on which I effectively 'collaged' sounds from the Internet by rearranging, distorting, looping and reinterpreting them. I also created the artwork for the cover.

STEP, personal project. Found imagery and pen on paper, 2015

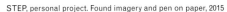

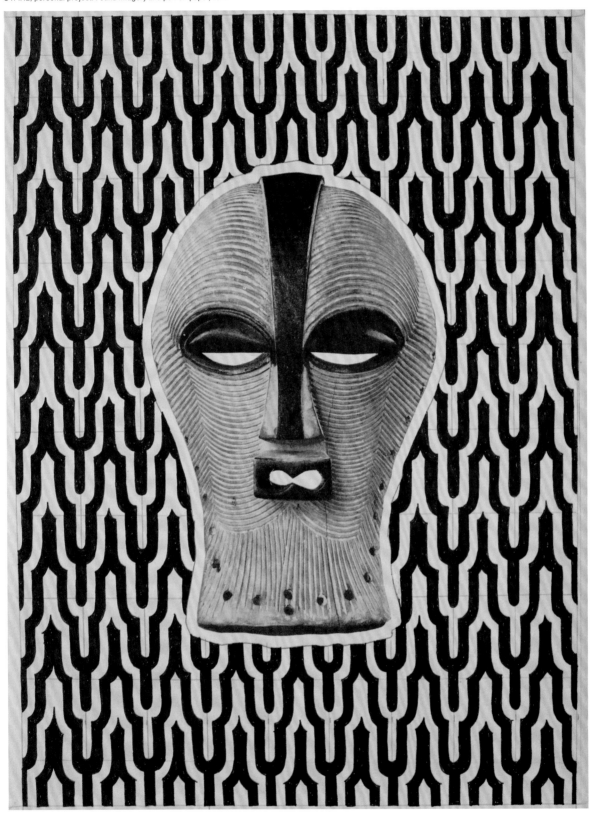

MATTHEW CRAVEN

MERIJN HOS

Merijn Hos is an artist and illustrator from Utrecht, the Netherlands. He divides his time between working as a commercial illustrator for well-known brands and publications (Coca-Cola, Red Bull, Pepsi, Nickelodeon, *Dazed & Confused* and *Wired*) and focusing on his own personal projects, exhibitions and independent publishing. His style fluctuates between analogue and digital, which gives his pieces a clean and graphic appearance, as well as a spontaneous feel. Specifically for his collage work, Hos retains this sense of freedom by refraining from sketching his ideas or compositions beforehand, preferring to work by trial and error.

POSTER FOR DOWN THE RABBIT HOLE. Handmade and digital collage, 2014

UNTITLED, for WeTransfer. Handmade and digital collage, 2013

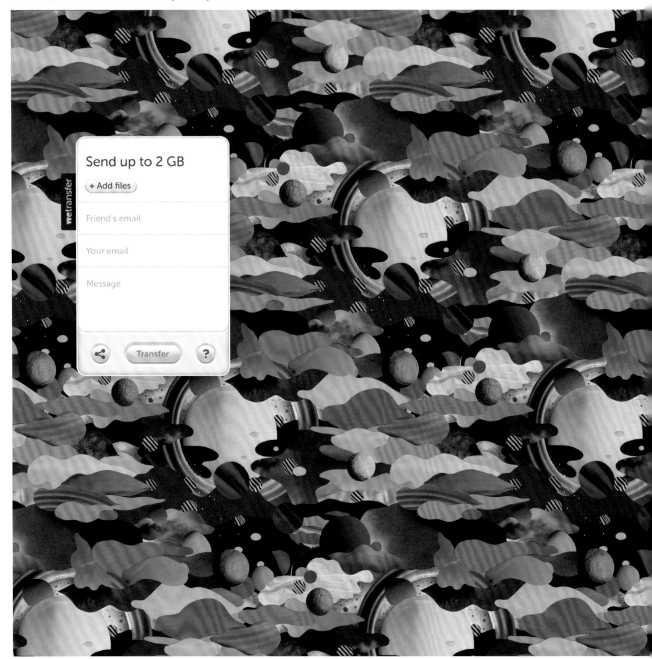

Artwork by Merijn Hos

Do you have a favourite collage?
I love John Stezaker's collages. They are so simple but cleverly made.

When did you first start making collages?
In Kindergarten, I think, but I started making collages professionally in around 2006. I'm not sure why I started but I remember it was a Saturday morning in Spring and I felt quite happy with the results.

And why do you think your initial attraction to collage has endured?
I love trialling various combinations of all the different pieces until the composition is right. I also love the fact that it is like painting without having to wait until the paint is dry.

Do you prefer to make collages digitally or by hand?
I use a mixture of handmade and digital techniques – somehow this works for me. I start out with a loose composition made by hand and then I tie everything together in Photoshop.

From where do you tend to source your imagery?
I use a lot of images from fashion magazines. I especially love to cut out close-ups of the fabrics.

Have you ever used anything unusual in a collage?
Nothing too unusual, but I love it when I find a piece of paper in the street with a nice colour or shape.

A LONG STRANGE TRIP, illustration for *Nylon Guys* magazine.
Handmade and digital collage, 2014

SUMMER ON THE FREEWAY, personal project. Handmade collage, 2014

MICHAEL HOLLAND

Manchester-based artist Michael Holland creates collages out of life's throwaway materials, rummaging through paper recycling and stacks of forgotten books to create handmade work that embraces the spirit of serendipity.

As well as creating collages for numerous event posters, Holland's work adorns the record, cassette and CD sleeves of releases from his own record label (Ono Records).

ALBUM COVER FOR *GLOSSOLALIA* by Brian Howe (Ono). Collage of record sleeves, postcards and passport photographs, 2008

ALBUM COVER FOR AVANT GARDE 3" by Andrew Hargreaves (Ono). Collage of record sleeves, postcards and passport photographs, 2008

Do you only ever make your collages by hand, or do you sometimes use digital techniques?
I always make them by hand. I'm not sure why, really, possibly just because of the immediacy – I like capturing the accidental and I dislike sitting at a computer when I'm meditating on something. Collage has always been a way for me to switch off: a way into another world.

When did you first come across collage?
When I was around eight years old, my dad showed me a book called *Dada and Surrealism Reviewed* by Dawn Ades, which gave me my first experience of collage. At that time, the artworks by Raoul Hausmann stood out for me most of all.

Do you have a favourite piece of design that uses collage?
The record sleeve for 'The Pictures on my Wall' by Echo and the Bunnymen springs to mind immediately, but I'm sure I could come up with a list as long as my arm.

Have you ever used anything unusual in a collage?
I mostly use paper but collage can incorporate anything. I've started to see most things as potential collages. For example, I've recently used clothes and even sounds.

What attracts you to the medium of collage?
I suppose collage is rubbish made beautiful. Historically, artists have tended to use materials that are in plentiful supply in their local area. I suppose I'm just following on that tradition, using the mess that surrounds us in the 21st century in its plentiful supply!

CASSETTE COVER FOR *ORPHIC RUIN* by Stress Waves (Ono). Risograph print, 2015

ALBUM ARTWORK FOR *LOOP PHANTASY NO. 2* by Stuart Chalmers (Ono). Risograph print, 2015

MIKE PERRY

Based in Brooklyn, New York, Mike Perry works within a vast range of media and formats. His collages teem with personality – they are full of distinctive and vibrant colour palettes, patterns, shapes and anthropomorphic objects. With an emphasis on the hand-drawn and the transformative power of craft, his style may appear childlike, but it also reminds viewers to find delight in art.

Perry has published several books on screen-printing and hand-drawn type and patterns. His commercial projects have seen him create work for Nike, Converse, Duvel, Urban Outfitters, Apple, Target, *New York Magazine* and *The New York Times*.

FORM FELT FEELING, personal project. Hand-cut paper, 2010

Opposite: SKETCH, from personal sketchbook. Hand-cut paper, 2012

SKETCH, from personal sketchbook. Hand-cut paper, 2012

194

MIKE PERRY

MIKE PERRY

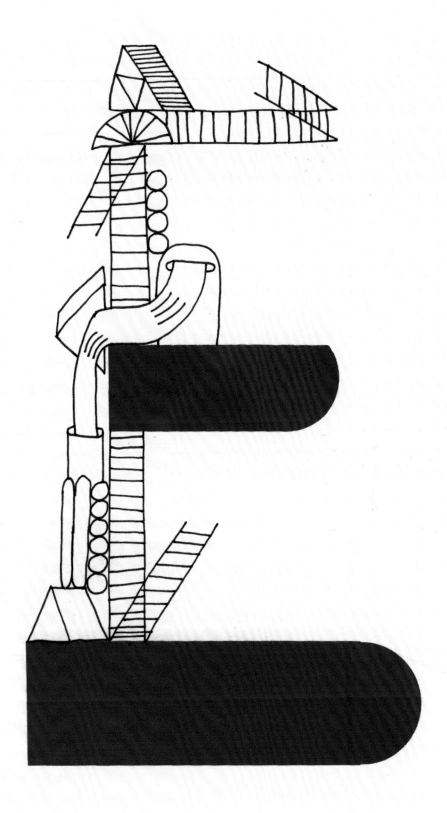

MIKE PERRY

What is your favourite piece of collage that you have made?
I love the zine entitled 'Lost in the Stacks' that I made in 2009
in collaboration with the New York Public Library. They pulled out
unusual books at my request and I made the entire zine from them.

From where do you tend to source your imagery?
I use whatever is lying around me. That said I have an entire flat-file
drawer filled with material for collages. Sometimes I pick up scraps
and slot them into my sketchbook. Then when I come to that page
I glue it down and try and make it into something.

Have you ever used anything unusual in one of your collages?
I think using cedar shingles to make a collage is pretty unusual.

MIRKO BORSCHE

In his role as Art Director at *Jetzt*, a German youth magazine, between 1999 and 2002, Mirko Borsche created a visual language that has since been imitated by many graphic designers. Producing numerous magazines, catalogues, books, posters, exhibition design and websites, all of his pieces consist of a concise idea and a very reduced number of elements. The few images present are usually collaged by hand, whilst the typography is contemporary without being self-consciously unconventional or edgy. In 2007, Borsche founded the Munich-based creative studio Bureau Mirko Borsche.

POSTER FOR BAYERISCHE STAATSOPER. Digital collage, 2014

BAYERISCHE STAATSOPER

FRAGMENT

Dienstag, 3. Juni 2014

DIE UNMÖGLICHE ENZYKLOPÄDIE № 29

ALLERHEILIGEN HOFKIRCHE   RESIDENZSTRASSE 1   BEGINN 20:00 UHR   EINLASS 19:45 UHR
KARTEN 8 EURO   INFORMATION / KARTEN   T 089.21 85 19 20   WWW.STAATSOPER.DE

CORPORATE IDENTITY FOR SEO SEO. Digital collage, 2014

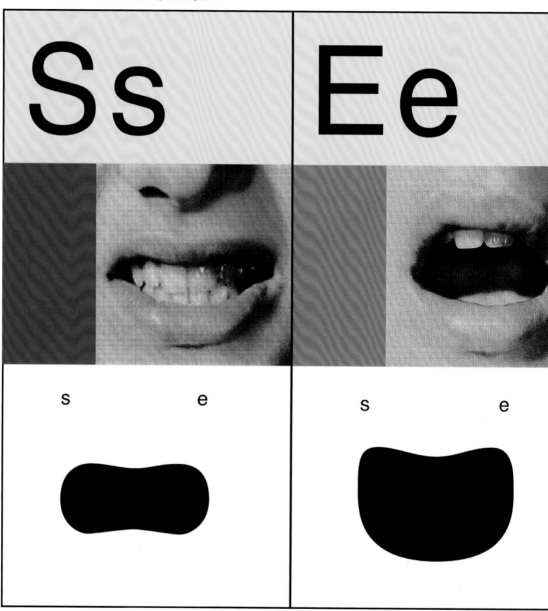

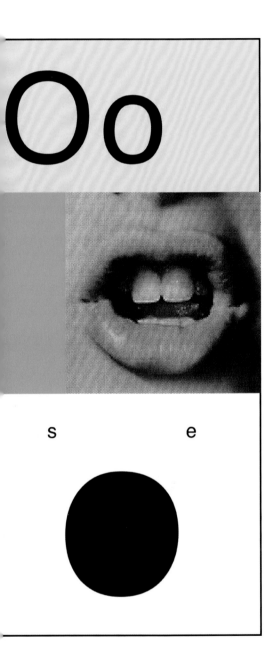

What do you think is the appeal of collage?
 On the one hand, it is a very difficult art form that only a few people can do with precision and success. On the other hand, anybody can do it regardless of whether the outcome is perfect, and it is a lot of fun.

Do you prefer to make collages digitally or by hand?
 By hand; it is much more fun, especially as I have to sit in front of the computer the rest of the time.

Do you recall when you first came across collage?
 In Kindergarten or maybe even before.

Have you ever used anything unusual in a collage?
 I do not think there is such a thing. In a collage, everything is possible.

SINGLE COVER FOR 'I MAKE YOU MAN'
by Telonius (Gomma). Handmade collage, 2014

MVM

Magnus Voll Mathiassen is a Norwegian independent graphic designer and illustrator whose work spans multiple disciplines and media and whose clients range from Adidas to the pop star Rihanna. He experiments with both handmade and digital collage, which sees him equally at home combining vector shapes as it does bringing together ink experiments with scans of marble surfaces. Many of his pieces emphasize abstraction and explore the natural juxtaposition of ugliness and joy within the world. There is a three-dimensional quality and an unfussy elegance to his collages: outlines pop and shadows are created by using lighter tones within block colours.

INNER RECORD SLEEVE FOR *SHADOW OF EVENTS*
by Alexander Rishaug (Dekorder). Digital collage, 2014

PROMOTIONAL POSTER FOR KUNST- OG KULTUR STRATEGI. Digital collage, 2014

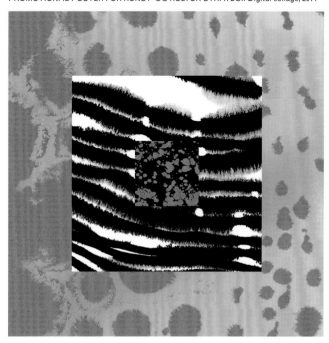

Overleaf: HOLIDAY CARD FOR HUGO & MARIE. Digital collage, 2014

When did you first come across collage?
  Doesn't every kid do some collage-ish pieces at one point? As for putting a label on such work, I must have been a young teenager when I read about the pop art movement and the term first came up.

From where do you tend to source your images?
  I usually use found images or images given to me by clients, which is then mixed with handmade material or archived illustrations.

Do you prefer to make collages digitally or by hand?
  At the moment my clients typically want something 'clean', so, unfortunately, my collages are usually made on the computer. Personally I like the gritty stuff – the simplicity and the happy accidents. And a hands-on approach is much more fun.

Do you have a favourite piece of design that uses collage in this gritty way?
  I think the whole punk and various underground rock scenes just did it the best. Raw. Photocopied. Rough. Dirty.

RECORD COVER FOR *SHADOW OF EVENTS* by Alexander Rishaug. Digital collage, 2014

MARBLEOUS, personal project. Digital collage, 2014

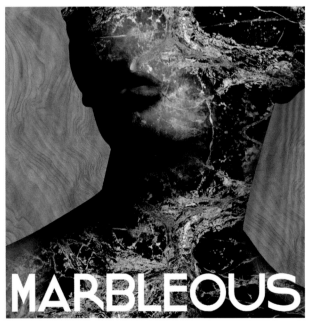

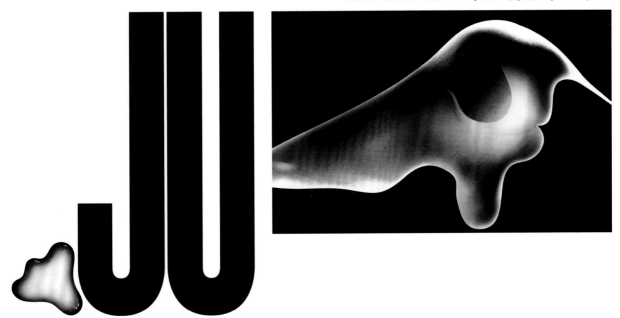

UNTITLED, for Granimator, a creative wallpaper app. Digital collage, 2014

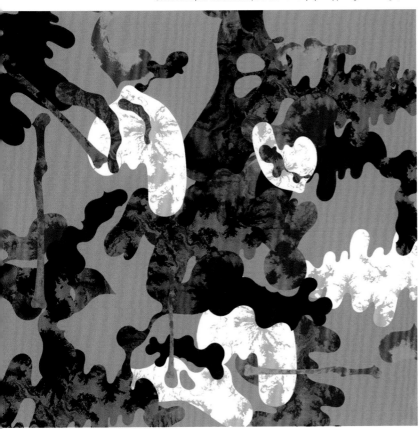

NARCSVILLE

A member of East London Printmakers since 2008, Narcsville is the studio of Nick Scott, a London-based creative whose brightly coloured creations have adorned the record sleeves and posters of The Cribs, Kate Nash, Wild Beasts and Domino Recording Company. Screen-printing is an integral part of the studio's design practice, as is a preference for handmade techniques and the use of cheap, second-hand materials to build each collage. The studio's illustrations on mental health for Vice UK (see below) are notable for their multiple layers and use of fluorescent colours, both of which are perfect for communicating visually the different elements of the human psyche.

RECORD BOOKLET ARTWORK FOR *IGNORE THE IGNORANT* by The Cribs (Wichita Recordings). Handmade collage, 2009

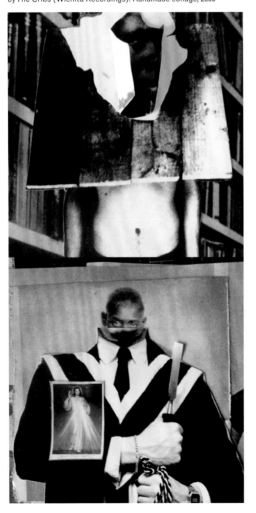

ILLUSTRATION ON MENTAL HEALTH for Vice UK. Digital collage, 2014

Do you have a favourite collage?
There are so many artists who have inspired me over the years:
Linder Sterling, Dash Snow, Art Chantry, John Stezaker, Peter
Kennard, Gee Vaucher, Tsunehisa Kimura, Julian House, Kate Gibb ...

When did you first come across collage?
Honestly? Probably the Peter Blake cover for the seven-inch copy
of Band Aid's 'Do They Know It's Christmas?' single, which, now
I think about it, was a really dark image for a five-year-old to be
studying. Then Richard Hamilton crept into my consciousness at
school, and Nirvana's *Incesticide* did the same at home. There was a
lot of work that looked like Raoul Hausmann's knocking about when
I was growing up in the early 1990s – it was much more a part of the
visual landscape back then. I didn't start making collages, though,
until I got to art school, and then I really went for it once I started
screen-printing.

From where do you tend to source your imagery?
Charity shops, thrift stores and junk markets are all good places,
but it really depends on the type of work I'm making. Collage has
become a part of my creative process but it's rarely the end result
of any project; it's more the thing I do for myself when not dealing
with clients and deadlines. When I make a collage for a commercial
project, I aim to shoot original imagery first that I will then use later
for the piece.

What's the strangest collage you've ever done?
I once did a series of collaged illustrations for The Cribs's album
Ignore The Ignorant, which required lots of my friends to strip down
and then dress up as figures of both power and oppression. I was
living in a tiny, damp flat in east London at the time, and I would
have these men come round, strip, wrap themselves up in hoods and
bin bags, and take dark, unpleasant images of them. One prop
I got my dad to make for me was this wooden neckpiece that was
like a mobile set of stocks, which my friend Joseph kindly wore in
a state of semi-undress. That wasn't a normal day at work.

Do you prefer to make your collages digitally or by hand?
I rarely make my collages digitally as it's too flexible and I need the
limitations. My favourite way of making collages is collaboratively.
I know that if I make something that is too derivative or wishy-washy,
my friend Louise Mason will either call me out on it or I'll see the
knowledge in her face that I can do better.

Besides the collaborative aspect of making collages, what attracts
you to this medium?
I love the immediacy of the process and the fact it takes away
control. What I can make is dictated by the materials I have to hand,
so it forces my brain to go in directions and shapes that aren't
always the easiest.

RECORD BOOKLET ARTWORK FOR *FOR ALL MY SISTERS*
by The Cribs (Sony Music). Screen-printed collage, 2015

RECORD BOOKLET ARTWORK FOR *FOR ALL MY SISTERS*
by The Cribs (Sony Music). Screen-printed collage, 2015

UNTITLED, personal project. Handmade collage using found imagery, 2014

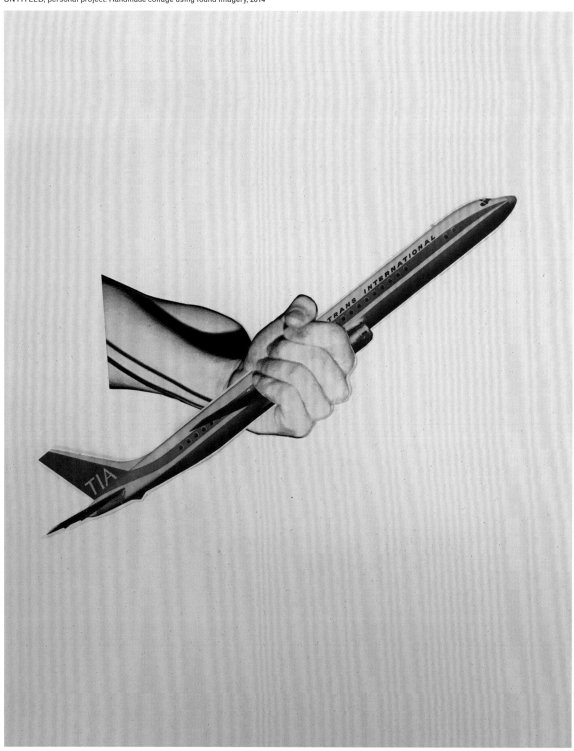

Opposite: AMERICAN LANDSCAPES, personal project.
Hand-cut collage and screen print, 2014

NEASDEN CONTROL CENTRE

Stephen Smith runs the London-based studio Neasden Control Centre, creating illustrations, typographic experiments, collages, sculptures and more for clients including Nike, Uniqlo and *Bloomberg Businessweek*. His collages consist largely of Matisse-esque shapes and scans or photographs of highly textured materials, giving his work a very distinct, handcrafted feel. His pieces are inherently contradictory in that they combine child-like shapes and a simple colour range with contemporary coolness – they exude both spontaneity and premeditated sleekness.

MONOCHROMATICITY, TR #303. B/W photocopy printed onto coloured paper, 2015

Top and bottom: MONOCHROMATICITY, TR #606. B/W photocopy printed onto coloured paper, 2015

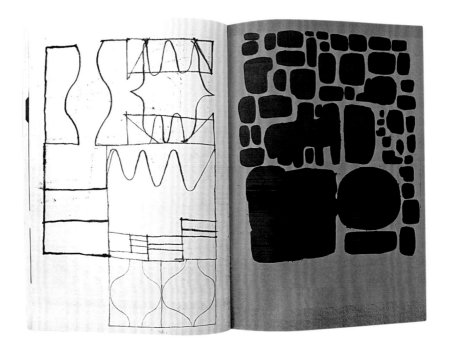

When did you first come across collage?
Collage is one of the first things you do with your hands even
if you don't realize at the time. It's the best tool in the bag.

Do you make your collages digitally or by hand?
I use a mixture of both. I also like to use some more unusual
methods, such as the triple-layer cutting technique.

From where do you tend to source your imagery?
I make my own imagery, either by printing, drawing, painting
or photocopying. From then onwards, I use collage techniques.

216

MONOCHROMATICITY, TR #808. B/W photocopy printed onto coloured paper, 2015

Opposite: MONOCHROMATICITY, TR #606.
B/W photocopy printed onto coloured paper, 2015

NICK MATTAN

Nick Mattan is a Belgian designer based in Antwerp whose collage work experiments with and conflates the boundaries between photography, illustration, typography, patterns and more. By encouraging this collision between different media and the handmade and the digital, Mattan creates his own visual language where various design elements from different worlds each vie for equal attention from the viewer. For his posters for Dutch furniture design collective Onbetaalbaar (see page 220), Mattan applies a consistent and relatable yet open-ended aesthetic, communicating above all the company's love for objects.

MY CHAIN HITS MY CHEST, personal project. Digital collage, 2014

ONBETAALBAAR FAIR FAIRE POSTER. Digital collage, 2015

What attracts you to the medium of collage?
  I like the luck factor: the random clicks on the computer that create accidental shapes and textures, or even dirty stains from my old scanner. You never have to start from a blank page; there is always something you can start messing around with.

From where do you tend to source your imagery?
  Scraps from experiments, old work, drawings and pictures from friends …

It sounds as though you use particularly tactile sources. Do you ever prefer to work digitally as opposed to handmade?
  For me, making the two meet is most interesting – having the handmade stuff with a more organic vibe clash with digital. And aren't all contemporary graphic designs collages in style or concept, if not in form? We all reinterpret each other's images, fonts, trends and shizzle.

Do you have a favourite collagist?
  I'm really obsessed with the video works of Alex Verhaest. The way she mixes animation, photography, video recordings and interactive technology with the themes and visual language of the Middle Ages blows me away. She shows us glimpses of our future whilst revisiting our history. That, to me, is the strength of a good collage, bringing new life into old ideas.

ONBETAALBAAR MECHELEN POSTER. Digital collage, 2015

ONBETAALBAAR BERCHEM POSTER. Digital collage, 2015

NICK MATTAN

RORSCHACH, personal project. Digital collage, 2013

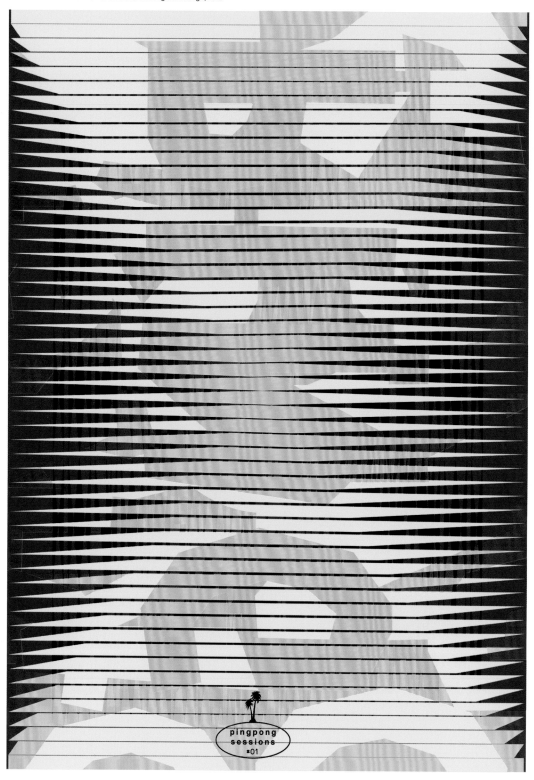

Opposite: BLACK ISLANDS CARPET,
personal project. Digital collage, 2014

NICK MATTAN

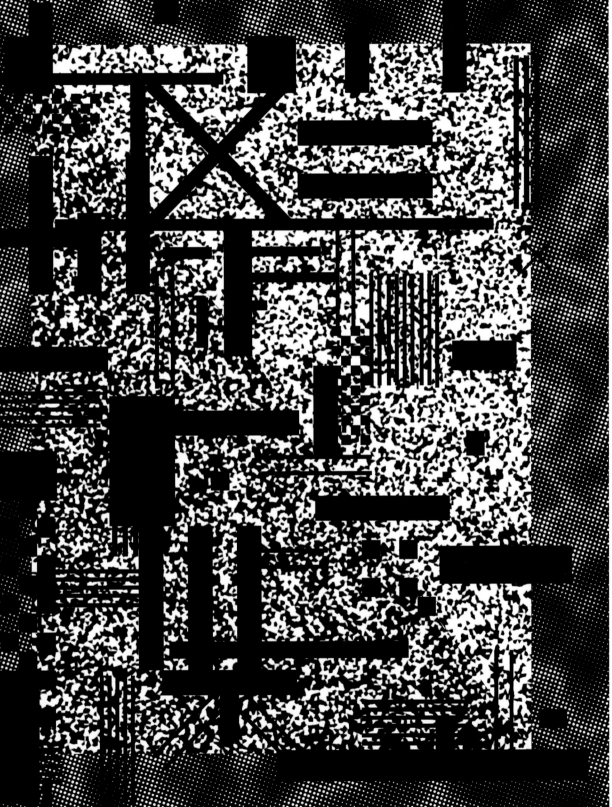

NOUS
VOUS

Comprising three creatives – Jay Cover, William Edmonds and Nicolas Burrows – Nous Vous works on a broad range of projects including illustration and graphic design commissions, exhibitions, curatorial work, publishing and teaching. The studio began in 2007 in Leeds, UK, where the trio met and studied together. Now based in London, collage is an integral part of their work, enabling them to test out various designs with speed. As a result, the images have a delightful, playful vitality to them, as well as an intriguing combination of colours, shapes and textures. Working by hand as much as possible, drawing is pivotal to their aesthetic, as is the use of 1980s-inspired, plastic-bright colours.

BOOK COVER FOR *MEET THE CIRCUS* by Edward Cheverton (Tate Publishing). Handmade collage using found materials, 2015

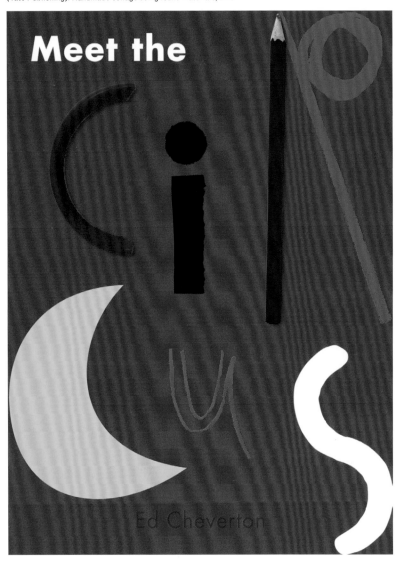

Opposite: RORBU for Little Paper Planes. Hand-cut collage, 2014

You work with a wide variety of media: painting, drawing, 3-D installation. Why does collage appeal to you?
  [Nicolas Burrows]: Collage is quick; it allows you to try out a wide variety of compositions. The simple gesture of placing a piece of paper, rather than, for example, transferring a pencil sketch into a painting, also gives the composition freshness.

Do you prefer to make collages digitally or by hand?
  It depends on the context. Each process is unique, so sometimes it is made digitally and sometimes by hand.

Have you ever used anything unusual in a collage?
  The beauty of collage is that you can use anything as your 'pieces' or materials. It's fun to mix them and to use surfaces and colours that go together well, so, in that respect, nothing in the process is unusual. We've made collages with household items, wood, fabric, photographs, metal ...

Opposite: 'VISITING TATE' BAG DESIGN
for Tate. Digital collage, 2015

schoolsandteachers@tate.org.uk
follow us on twitter @tateteachers
020 7887 8888
tate.org.uk

TATE

PAUL SAHRE

Famous for his book cover designs, record sleeve covers and illustrations for *The New York Times*, Paul Sahre established his own design consultancy in New York in 1997. His style is confident and humorous, and, particularly with regard to his editorial illustrations, he tends to use a combination of photography and found imagery to create visual one-liners (see page 231). Although Sahre's very early work can be identified by its extensive use of silk-screening (employed at a time when the technique was largely considered obsolete), his more recent work tends to eschew categorization and is reactionary by nature.

ALBUM COVER FOR *NANOBOTS* by They Might Be Giants (Lojinx). Handmade collage using found imagery, 2013

Opposite: THE HOCKEY NEWS. Hand-cut collage, 2012

Expansion as Draft P...

Hockey News

INTERNATIONAL HOCKEY WEEKLY

VOL. 32 NO. 35, JULY, 1979   64522 $1.00

NHL SETS 'ENTRY'

outspo... coach is ...omplish... Denver... looked ...ell gua... ...chise in ...

year w... good fo... players... I like th... ther, the... their best... year end... Bo...

...s hit the ...and Ran-... ...yers will ...e the star-... Quebec ...art from ...old Dave

— Page 9

Was it the fans; the owners; the scorecard manufacturers?

A total of 65 players were juggled around in the space of three and a half hours in the NHL's fifth expan-

15 PAGES OF STATISTICS THE INSIDE

...pained ...other 17...

SABRES TO DO IT BOWMAN'S WAY

— Page 2

CHERRY'S RIPE ROCKIES

...yard, signed one ...ree agent.

...eer lacking ...n talk of fol-... ...rrouded the

...e for real,'' ...Pohan smi-... ...e something ...franchise is ...e of day-to-... ...since A-P-A ...by Arthur ...team from ...ers late last

...von only 15 ...llion in their ...outlook was ...announced ...play in Den-... ...weeks later ...Cherry had

...on, recently ...r contract, ...ems Cherry ...ins' front-... ...escribes the ...coach who ...d.''

...lly humble ...ates. ''When ...barrassed,'' ...an't get the ...care who's ...s, you can't

player, Cherry continued. "I like the talent here. My son likes fishing. I like the outdoors and I like the challenge.

"My family decided it almost for me," Cherry said. "I wanted to accept the challenge (of transforming the worst team in the NHL into a contender). They seemed to be more enthusiastic about Denver than any other team."

Miron contacted Cherry the day after he parted ways with the Bruins. Miron then met with Bill Watters, a representa-... ...een mentioned for this position, A... MacNeil is the only man I had in mind."

"I am delighted to have the opportu-

...rthy Wall

...Year Deal As Coach

...of the franchise outside of the draf... ...of Barry Beck. It's the most impor... ...thing this year, even more import... ...than how we use the first-round dr... ...pick. His philosophy is to have fun a... ...work hard at the same time. A li... ...more hard work won't hurt this tea... ...''And neither will Cherry.''

CENT...

NHL JERS...

In an important player signing ...patience finally paid off for the Atlanta Flames when they acquired the contrac... of super-scorer Kent Nilsson from the Winnipeg Jets.

A fourth round draft pick of the Fla... mes back in 1976, Nilsson opted to sign ...with the Jets and in two short seasons ...has quickly proven that he is one of the ...finest offensive threats that the spor... has to offer.

In his first season, he scored ...in one

...signing) get the fans' interest. I'm sure we'll have a sound system this time. The way Don has coached, if you don't play his system, you don't play.''

''If anyone can shape this outfit up, he'd be the one who can do it,'' added defenseman Mike Christie. ''I think it's the most important thing in the history

FACE-OFF GAME

...y season this coming fall

"... the finest sports tablegame which I have ever played." This is how one purchaser described FACE-OFF. Now you can experience the same exciting action! Over 400 skater and goalie cards are included in the game. These cards reflect the performance of each player in the most recent season. The following are a sample of the various ratings:

SHOOTING: Home and Away   DEFENSIVE ABILITY

SCORING: Including short-handed and power-play goals

PASSING, FACE-OFF, FORECHECKING, and SHOT-BLOCKING ABILITY

INTIMIDATION and PENALTIES (includes both type and frequency)

ASSISTS   INJURIES   DURABILITY/FATIGUE

PERFORMANCE RATING: Frequency of Player Usage

Goalies ... for you just as they did in real life, making key saves, controlling rebounds, and even incurring penalties.

FACE-OFF provides the gamer with the opportunity to direct his or her favorite team. It combines an explicitly detailed instruction ...s most frequently used lines/defense pairings) for a truly complete game. One can even form draft-type leagues, experiencing little distortion in statistical accuracy.

Should you require additional information regarding FACE-OFF, we have a brochure which discusses the game in more depth. Or you can get right to the heart of the matter by ordering the actual FACE-OFF rulebook. You can then determine the exact nature of the game.

Get in on the great hockey action of FACE-OFF. Order today. Newest edition available September 15th of each year. Send check/ money order in U.S. currency only.

CONFRO, INC.   P.O. BOX 345   BLOOMINGTON, IL 61701
....$ 22.9...

FERGIE WAITS

JETS GRAB HULL BACK HAWKS

EDMONTON—Mike ...ler, Bryon Baltimore, Bry... ...and Dave Fortier, defens... ...Thomas, Dave Forbes.

— Page 3

...yard, claimed from Cincinnati, Bob ...the 19... draft, org

...ds Berry, Smith 'Rockies'

...ott; Terry ...ffalo; Jamie ...St. Louis; ...52 from ...DENVER—... ...s, moving to ...ward lines, ...enter Doug ...and signed ...inger Barry

...e Rockies' ...arry Beck in ...sign with the ...key Associa-... ...nt much of ...tral Hockey ...eviously, the ...und Berry ...the Univer-...

...who was a ...the Boston

two players. ''Barry Smith plays both center and left wing and Doug Berry had a pretty good year in Dal-las. We're getting two good, young players.

''Don (Cherry) recommended Smith. He's not a goal-scorer. He's a good checker, more of a defensive player.'' Miron said of the five-foot-11, 186-pound Smith.

...RET'S ...ITAGE

''His all-around game is pretty good. His only drawback is his ska-ting,'' Miron continued.

Miron feels that the year of expe-

THE TOP DEFENDER

Denis Potvin of the Islanders won the Norris Trophy again as the NHL's and Dave Lumley ... Potvin shared the awards' limelight with seve-ral other NHL stars. For details see page 19.

Photo by Steve Babineau

...Up front, the Oiler... ...particularly well. Their ...the entire draft was Ca... ...who scored two goals

NHL'S FINAL PLUS-MINUS STATISTICS

— Pages 22-23

DESIGN MATTERS!. Silkscreen-printed collage, 2009

Do you have a favourite collagist?
Favourite as in 'all-time'? John Heartfield. Easily the greatest collage artist ever. He helped invent collage AND he deployed his invention against Hitler.

What attracts you to the medium of collage?
It's quick. It's gestural. In a way, graphic designers are collage artists from the outset; they typically take things from multiple sources to create something new.

Does graphic design play a greater hand in your collage work, or do you also use handmade techniques?
I use a combination of methods. The final work of art is almost always digital, though.

From where do you tend to source your original images?
Anywhere, but mostly through my personal library – I've been collecting odd books for content and visual reference for years. Here are a few random titles: *Eaton's Fall and Winter Catalogue*, *Yoga Tennis*, *International Symposium on Amphetamines and Related Compounds*, *The Complete Book of Jets and Rockets*, *What is Water?*, *College Typing (Second Edition)*, *Christmas Ideals Quarterly*, *Boobytraps: Department of the Army Field Manual* and *The Secret Of Eternal Life*.

Of all the materials you've used previously, is there one that particularly stands out?
I once forced a typography class at the School of Visual Arts to make collages for an entire semester using a single issue of *The Hockey News* that I found in my dad's attic after he passed away. Each student only used the issue they were given (all from the years between 1973 and 1980) for a variety of projects. By the end all they had was a stripped-down skeleton of a newspaper.

REAL W.M.D'S for *The New York Times Book Review* cover. Digital collage using found imagery, 2008

The New York Times
Book Review

June 22, 2008

Copyright © 2008 The New York Times

OFFICE OF PAUL SAHRE

Real W.M.D.'s

By Richard Holbrooke

ONE MINUTE TO MIDNIGHT Kennedy, Khrushchev, and Castro on the Brink of Nuclear War. *By Michael Dobbs. Illustrated. 426 pp. Alfred. A. Knopf. $28.95.*

Any new entry in the crowded field of books on the 1962 Cuban missile crisis must pass an immediate test: Is it just another recapitulation, or does it increase our net understanding of this seminal cold war event? By focusing on the activities of the American, Soviet and Cuban militaries during those tense October days, Michael Dobbs's "One Minute to Midnight" passes this test with flying colors. The result is a book with sobering new information about the world's only superpower nuclear confrontation — as well as contemporary relevance.

Dobbs, a reporter for The Washington Post, states his central thesis concisely in a description of the state of play on Oct. 25, the 10th day of the crisis: "The initial reactions of both leaders had been bellicose. Kennedy had favored an air strike; Khrushchev thought seriously about giving his commanders in Cuba

Continued on Page 8

LEAH HAGER COHEN: ROXANA ROBINSON'S 'COST' **PAGE 5** | JAY McINERNEY: ANDRE DUBUS III'S 'GARDEN OF LAST DAYS' **PAGE 7**

PAUL SAHRE

EARTH RISE for *The New York Times*. Handmade collage using found imagery, 2008

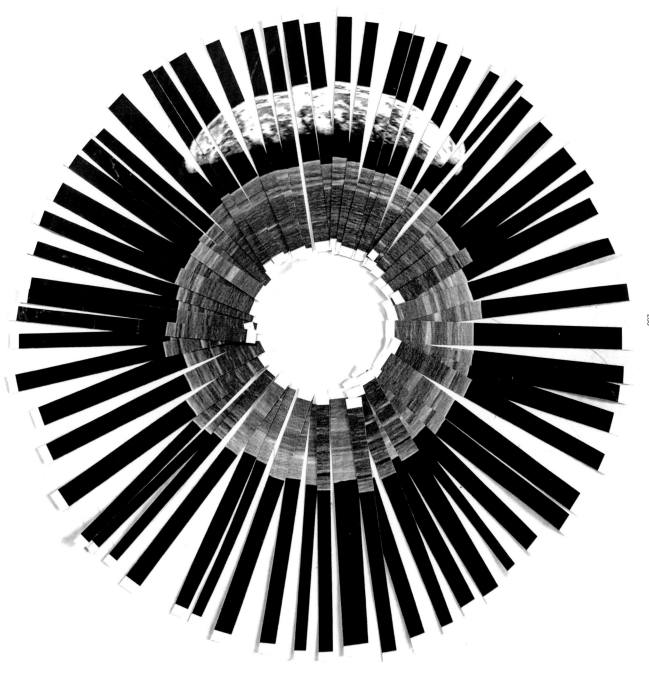

PAUL SAHRE

ROBERT BEATTY

Kentucky-based Robert Beatty is an artist and musician who creates work that transports the viewer to digital, otherworldly and often dystopian landscapes. Famous for his record sleeve designs for Tame Impala, The Phantom Band and Steve Moore (as well as for his own musical projects: Three Legged Race, Hair Police and Burning Star Core), Beatty's aesthetic stands out from the rest of his contemporaries. It is most reminiscent of the mind-bending, hallucinatory album covers that were ubiquitous during the 1970s, but Beatty's use of computerized techniques and geometric patterns to achieve this appearance places his work firmly in the 21st century.

CASSETTE COVER FOR *ROPE COMMERCIAL VOL. 2* by Three Legged Race (Vitrine). Digital collage, 2015

ALBUM COVER FOR *RAINBOW ARABIA* by F.M. Sushi (Time No Place). Digital collage, 2013

ROBERT BEATTY

When did you first come across collage?
I'm sure it was in art class in elementary school. I remember cutting
images out of my mom's *True Story* magazines when I was a kid and
pasting them together, but I don't remember anything specific that I made.

What attracts you to the medium of collage?
I like the flexibility and freedom to change things around easily. One
move in one direction or the other and you can create a completely
different feeling. I like the element of chance: the act of throwing the
pieces out and seeing where they land.

Whose collages do you particularly enjoy?
I love Eduardo Paolozzi's screenprints, Jeff Keen's films, Bruce
Conner's photo collages, Tadanori Yokoo's posters, Julian House's
record covers … I could go on, but those are some of my favourites.

From where do you tend to source your imagery?
I usually create everything from scratch, whether it's photos or original
artwork. Even if I want to reference something that exists already, I
prefer to recreate it myself just so it differs from the original.

Afterwards, do you prefer to work digitally or by hand?
I like both, but I tend to work digitally because that's how everything
ends up these days, anyway.

Have you ever used anything unusual in a collage?
I've done things with some pretty bizarre found photos, but nothing that
anyone's seen, really. I worked as a janitor at a truck stop for a few years
and would always find crazy photos in the trash.

COVER FOR *RAPPER TURNED SINGER* EP by Andy Petr (Mixpak Records). Digital collage, 2011

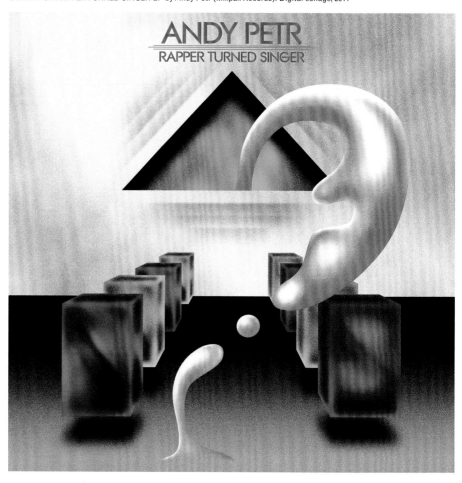

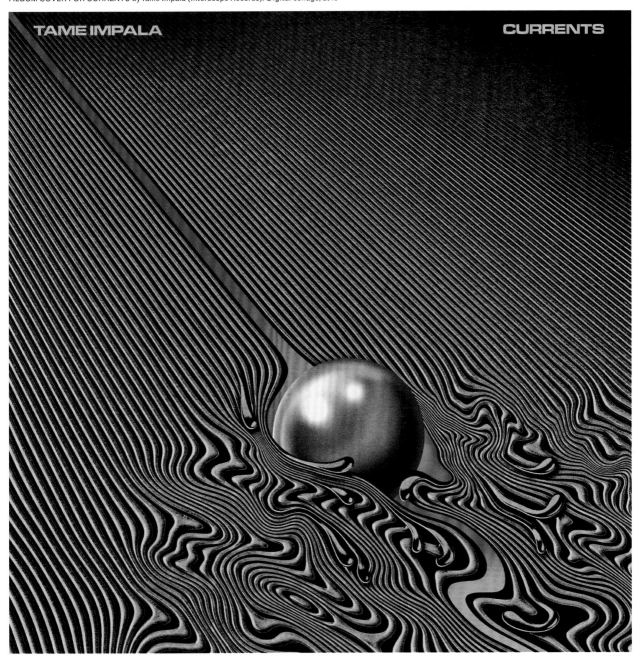

ALBUM COVER FOR *A CONSTANT MOTH* by Lord RAJA (Ghostly International). Digital collage, 2014

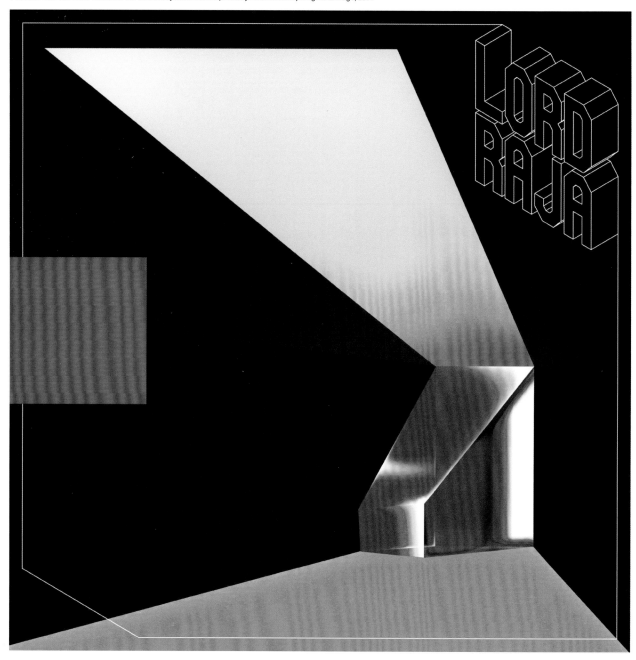

ALBUM COVER FOR *PANGAEA ULTIMA* by Steve Moore (Spectrum Spools). Digital collage, 2013

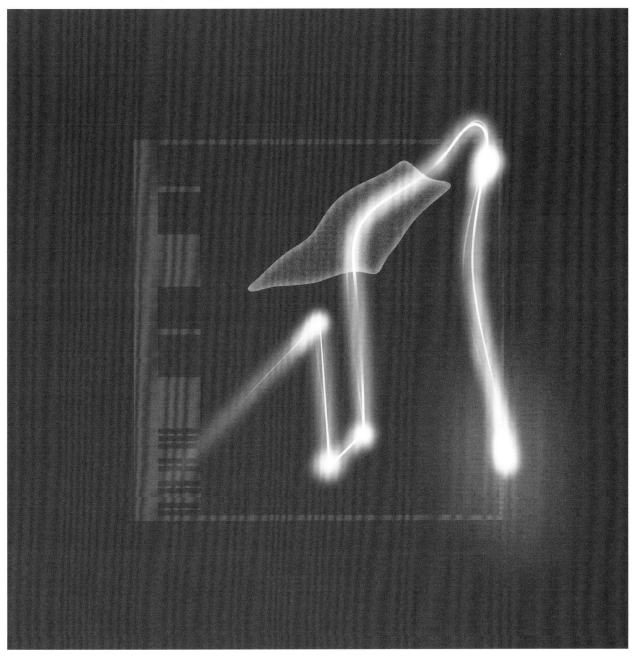

RONNY
HUNGER

Ronny Hunger is a graphic artist based in Zürich, Switzerland. Since 2009 he has created posters, packaging, books and publications for commercial clients in cultural fields. Hunger is known for making extensive use of the screen-printing process, which serves to highlight the cut-and-paste, DIY style of his collages. His posters typically combine found imagery, hacked graphic symbols and experimental typography to create multiple visual layers that mirror the music they are promoting.

POSTER FOR NO AGE GIG at Palace St.Gallen. Handmade collage, 2013

POSTER FOR WHITE FENCE'S EUROPEAN TOUR. Handmade collage, 2013

POSTER FOR DUCKTAILS GIG at Elmo Delmo. Handmade collage, 2013

When did you first come across collage?
When I first saw my father's record collection.

Do you have an all-time favourite collage design?
I couldn't possibly decide on a favourite because there's so much out there. But I am really into almost all the collage work by my friends Damien Tran and Marion Jdanoff from Palefroi, as well as Nadine Nakanishi and Nick Butcher from Sonnenzimmer.

What draws you to collage?
With collage you can combine entirely different worlds to form one big image. I take my images from multiple sources: books, magazines, the Internet, hand drawings and 3D CAD software.

With such a wide range of source material, do you prefer to make collages digitally or by hand?
Both of them are good. It doesn't matter which you prefer – it's more important why you choose one of these methods and whether it matches your actual idea. The content is more important than the technique.

Have you ever used anything unusual in a collage?
There's no such thing as 'unusual' in collage – everything is possible.

ALBUM COVER FOR *ALL SHIP SHAPE*
by Dri#ter (Coldkings). Handmade collage, 2013

POSTER FOR JESSICA PRATT GIG at Elmo Delmo. Handmade collage, 2014

JULIA
HOLTER

Julia Holter (USA)

POSTER FOR VINTAGE GANT N°2. Handmade collage, 2014

Vintage Gant N°2
Versteigerung von Vintage Objekten

13. Dezember 2014
Café Bar Treppenhaus, Rorschach

ALBUM COVER FOR *IT'S A PRESSURE TO MEET YOU*
by Odd Couple (not on label). Handmade collage, 2013

ODD COUPLE
It's A Pressure
To Meet You

Opposite: POSTER FOR JULIA HOLTER GIG at Palace
St.Gallen. Handmade collage and screen print, 2013

SANTTU MUSTONEN

Santtu Mustonen is a Finnish artist based in Brooklyn, New York, whose clients range from *The New York Times*, *Wired* and Granta Books to Nike and Converse. The phrase 'colourful mud' is sometimes used to describe his work. Inspired by organic patterns, natural science, 3-D design and movement, Mustonen uses a 3-D modelling programme to digitally animate various hand-crafted textures and paintings and conjure a fantastical world. As a result, his pieces are hypnotic, rhythmic, joyous and bewildering. His use and range of colour appears to know no bounds – explosions, spills and trails of paint stream across the pages.

When did you first come across collage?
Professionally, the first time I opened Photoshop.

Do you prefer to make your collages digitally or by hand?
For me, both methods are important. Often I will start working by hand and finish the piece digitally – or the other way around.

What attracts you to the medium of collage?
I'm interested in combining shapes and colours that are not naturally connected.

From where do you tend to source your imagery?
I tend to use cell-phone photographs and video clips, or my own intuitive painting and mark-making.

OREGON CHAIN BLADE, personal project. Digital collage, 2014

Opposite: BALLBEARINGS, personal project. Digital collage, 2015

SEBASTIAN HASLAUER

Sebastian Haslauer is a Berlin-based artist and illustrator whose handmade collages delight in the absurd and the farthest reaches of the imagination. Their impact on the viewer is immediate: they combine found imagery, painting and roughly cut-out, coloured shapes in an overtly spontaneous way. Haslauer has created commercial projects for companies such as Nike, *Neon – A Literary Magazine* and numerous record labels. He has published many art books and fanzines, and often collaborates with Hort (see page 76), another Berlin-based creative studio, to give workshops in educational institutions.

MEMENTO MONI. Acrylic, paper and enamel on canvas, 2012

Opposite: URLAUB IN GEBERLÄNDERN. Acrylic, paper and enamel on canvas, 2012

BUCO DELL'OZONO (CONCETTO SPAZIALE). Paper collage, 2014

What attracts you to collage?
On the one hand, I love collaging because it is such a playful method and you can work very fast and spontaneously. This makes it a very powerful, immediate technique. On the other hand, it is difficult to create depth and develop a distinctive artistic handwriting.

Do you have a favourite collage?
Nothing springs to my mind at the moment, but I don't think collage is particularly good for illustrating or designing things, anyway, as it is not very precise. You are dependent on your material and what you manage to find. Commissioned collages can become very exhausting if your client has a specific image that needs to appear in the work. Personally I am mostly enthusiastic about more abstract collages. Currently, my favourite collagist is Chris Harnan. I have two amazing works of his hanging in my flat. And Sergei Sviatchenko is, with every right, the crowned king of collage.

Do you prefer to make collages digitally or by hand?
Strictly by hand. It has far more charm. And the computer already eats up too much of my time.

What's the most unusual thing you've included in one of your collages?
I once used my wisdom tooth in my piece *Setzkasten* [see page 257].

REOPENING OF THE BAVARIAN STATE OPERA. Paper collage, 2014

BAKAL. Acrylic and paper collage, 2014

KOPI. Acrylic and paper collage, 2014

QOTON. Acrylic and paper collage, 2014

TRANSIT. Paper collage, 2014

SETZKASTEN. Teeth, plastic and paper collage, 2014

STAHL R

Stahl R is a Berlin-based design studio founded in 2012 by Tobias Röttger and Susanne Stahl. Before starting up the studio, Röttger also worked for Hort (see page 76) for a number of years. Stahl R uses both its own and found imagery to compose its collages, with pattern frequently providing the centrepiece and communicating the central concept for the overall design. With a broad range of clients from commercial and cultural fields, including IBM, Microsoft, Adidas, Amnesty International and the Bavarian State Opera, the studio's design solutions are predominantly research- and concept-driven rather than adhering to a single and identifiable aesthetic across all projects.

SINGLE COVER FOR 'CALI IN LOVE' by Lemos and Tonny Lasar (Resopal). Part of the 'Resopal Series' project. Handmade collage, 2012

COVER FOR THE BRAND BOOK FOR MAZINE. Handmade collage, 2013

COVER FOR THE BRAND BOOK FOR MAZINE. Handmade collage, 2013

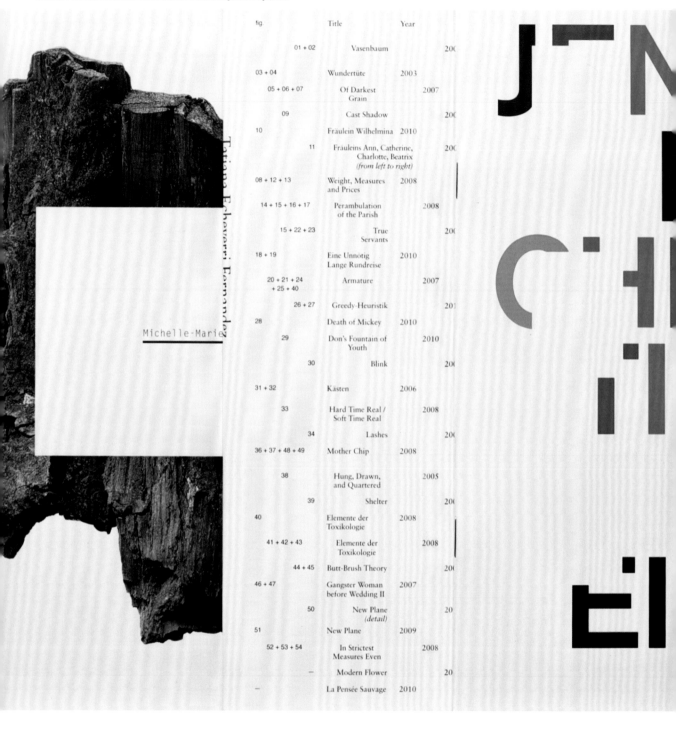

COVER FOR THE GOLDRAUSCH CATALOGUES. Digital collage, 2013

fig.	Title	Year	
01 + 02	Vasenbaum		200
03 + 04	Wundertüte	2003	
05 + 06 + 07	Of Darkest Grain	2007	
09	Cast Shadow		200
10	Fräulein Wilhelmina	2010	
11	Fräuleins Ann, Catherine, Charlotte, Beatrix *(from left to right)*		200
08 + 12 + 13	Weight, Measures and Prices	2008	
14 + 15 + 16 + 17	Perambulation of the Parish	2008	
15 + 22 + 23	True Servants		200
18 + 19	Eine Unnötig Lange Rundreise	2010	
20 + 21 + 24 + 25 + 40	Armature	2007	
26 + 27	Greedy-Heuristik		201
28	Death of Mickey	2010	
29	Don's Fountain of Youth	2010	
30	Blink		200
31 + 32	Kästen	2006	
33	Hard Time Real / Soft Time Real	2008	
34	Lashes		200
36 + 37 + 48 + 49	Mother Chip	2008	
38	Hung, Drawn, and Quartered	2005	
39	Shelter		200
40	Elemente der Toxikologie	2008	
41 + 42 + 43	Elemente der Toxikologie	2008	
44 + 45	Butt-Brush Theory		200
46 + 47	Gangster Woman before Wedding II	2007	
50	New Plane *(detail)*		20
51	New Plane	2009	
52 + 53 + 54	In Strictest Measures Even	2008	
—	Modern Flower		20
—	La Pensée Sauvage	2010	

Tatiana Echeverri Fernandez

Michelle-Marie

What attracts you to the practice of making collages?
 [Tobias Röttger]: The moment when you combine elements to create
 something wholly unexpected is quite magical.

From where do you find these initial elements?
 Sometimes found imagery but we mostly use our own.

Do you have a preference for working either digitally or by hand?
 Working with your hands is a much more fulfilling process, but,
 of course, the computer helps maintain an economical workflow.

Have you ever used any unusual sources in one of your collages?
 In my university days I used things like felt and fur, but I couldn't
 find proper ways to digitize them for further usage.

SINGLE COVER FOR 'THE MERCY DUBZ' by Echologist feat. The Spaceape (Resopal). Digital collage, 2009

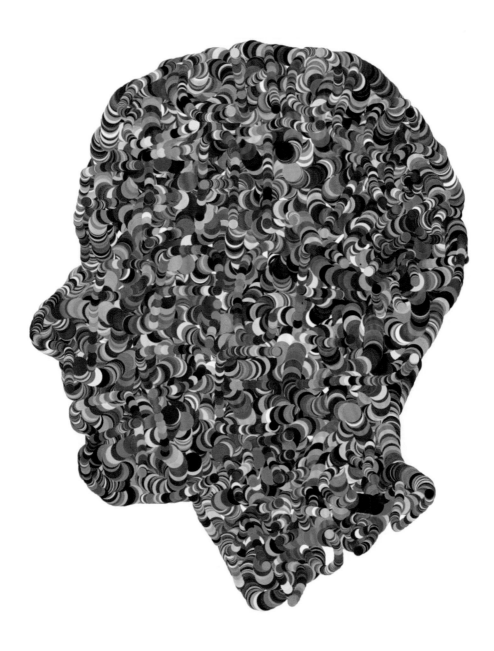

RECORD COVER FOR *BACK UP 3*, compilation album by various artists (Resopal). Digital collage, 2013

STEFAN SAGMEISTER

Austrian-born Stefan Sagmeister resides in New York where he co-runs the design firm Sagmeister & Walsh with Jennifer Walsh. Sagmeister's collages are typical of the rest of his artistic output: provocative and highly conceptual. Although his techniques are often simple to the point of banality, the resulting works are unsettling in their uncharacteristic combination of sensationalism, humour, sexuality and unease.

Sagmeister has amassed an enviable list of clients, including Talking Heads, the Rolling Stones, Lou Reed and the Guggenheim Museum, and he has had his work exhibited all around the world from Seoul to Prague.

POSTER FOR AIGA in New Orleans.
Handmade collage using found imagery, 1997

STEFAN SAGMEISTER

POSTER FOR FRESH DIALOGUE. Handmade collage using found imagery and ink, 1996

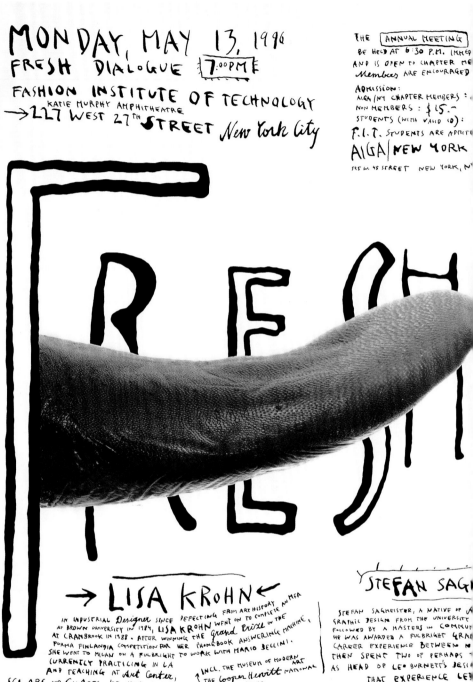

266

STEFAN SAGMEISTER

CHAPTER WILL
FRESH DIALOGUE.
ALL CHAPTER
TO PARTICIPATE.

argl

THE MISSION OF THE NEW YORK CHAPTER OF THE AMERICAN INSTITUTE OF GRAPHIC ARTS (AIGA/NY) IS TO IDENTIFY AND DEFINE CRITICAL ISSUES TO THE MEMBERSHIP AND THE GRAPHIC DESIGN PROFESSION; TO EXPLORE AND CLARIFY THESE ISSUES FOR THE PURPOSE OF HELPING TO ELEVATE THE STANDARDS OF GRAPHIC DESIGN; TO CREATE DESIGN BUSINESS PRACTICE AND THE ART OF GRAPHIC DESIGN; A FORUM FOR THE EXCHANGE OF INFORMATION, VIEWS, STYLE, AND TECHNIQUES AMONG THOSE ENGAGED IN THE PROFESSION.
THE AIGA/NY GRATEFULLY ACKNOWLEDGES ITS PARTNERS IN DESIGN FOR THEIR SIGNIFICANT CONTRIBUTIONS AND CONTINUING SUPPORT OF OUR EDUCATIONAL PROGRAMS.
NATIONAL REPROGRAPHICS INC., NEW YORK, NY; SPEED GRAPHICS, INC., NY, NY;
TYPOGRAM, INC., NEW YORK, NY;
VOMELA SYSTEM GRAPHICS, NEW YORK AND ST. PAUL.

DIALOGUE

| io 360 |

→ IN LESS THAN 2 YEARS, io 360 HAS BUILT ONE OF THE HOTTEST NEW MULTI-DISCIPLINARY DESIGN STUDIOS WORKING IN A VARIETY OF MEDIA ENVIRONMENTS. IT'S WORK BLENDS DISCIPLINES AS WIDE RANGING AS PHOTOGRAPHY, ARCHITECTURE AND PROGRAMMING TO PROJECTS RANGING FROM WEB SITES (THEY DEVELOPED THE FIRST INTERNET-BASED GAME SHOW) TO VIDEO GRAPHICS, CUSTOM INTERFACE DESIGN AND CD-ROM DEVELOPMENT. THEY HAVE BUILT A CLIENT LIST INCLUDING MAJOR ENTERTAINMENT, PUBLISHING, ADVERTISING AND TELECOMMUNICATION COMPANIES AS WELL AS MUSEUMS AND EVEN AN ORCHESTRA.
I.D. MAGAZINE AWARDED io 360 THE DESIGN DISTINCTION AWARD FOR INTERACTIVE DESIGN AND THEY WERE INCLUDED IN THIS YEAR'S I.D. TOP 40. WITH A BELIEF THAT TECHNOLOGY CREATES NEW OPPORTUNITIES FOR EXPRESSION AND COMMUNICATION, io 360 IS BOTH TECHNICALLY SAVVY AND TECHNOLOGY DRIVEN.

R/
ED A MFA IN
IN VIENNA
FROM Pratt INSTITUTE.
ND SPLIT HIS EARLY
TIVE YEARS OF HIS CAREER
VIENNA. SAGMEISTER
HONG KONG.
TO New York WHERE, AFTER
ISTER INC. IN 1993.
T",
LOU REED,
D the
GN

DESIGN: SAGMEISTER INC.
PHOTO: TOM SCHIERLITZ
PREPRESS:)
STALL PLOCH & THE IMAGING CONSORTIUM
PRINTING: L.P. THEBAULT COMPANY
C-PRINTS & FILM PROCESSING: COLOREDGE NYC.

PAPER: S.D. WARREN LUSTRO DULL, 80LB TEXT

STEFAN SAGMEISTER

ABRAMS

THINGS I HAVE LEARNED

STEFAN SAGMEISTER

Do you prefer to make collages digitally or by hand?
  My preference is handmade. Because I'm fifty-three.

Describe how the idea for the cover of your book *Things I Have Learned in My Life So Far* (see opposite) came about.
  I had designed a die-cut slipcase prototype for a project for Vitra, which ultimately never went ahead. I then applied a variation of that concept to the design of an annual for the Graduate School of Architecture, Planning and Preservation at Columbia University. Although conceptually it did not work for the School, I became interested in the idea of a cover in which you could insert single, interchangeable booklets, which would then operate as a kind of interactive collage.

Later on, I developed this idea for a publication featuring my own work. Originally I used drawings of toast and legs, but it became apparent that I needed a strong visual focus point to unify the various booklet covers. It was only when I replaced the drawings of toast with a photographic portrait that the cover came together properly. The different booklets allowed for 16 different covers in the bookstore (wonderful displays were made with it!) and a wide variety of reading experiences.

Opposite: BOOK COVER FOR *THINGS I HAVE LEARNED IN MY LIFE SO FAR* by Stefan Sagmeister (Abrams). Headshot with die-cut sections through which various covers using found imagery appear, 2008

STEFAN SAGMEISTER

STEVE HOCKETT

Steve Hockett is a graphic designer and illustrator based in Manchester, UK, who runs the creative studio Wonder Room. Using a combination of analogue and digital techniques, he specializes in posters and record sleeves, with a focus on the interplay between imagery and typography. One central concern is how to give mediums originally designed for print new lives in digital formats – particularly on social media. This is largely achieved through the pervading sense of movement in many of his collages. As well as creating material for independent music acts and venues, Hockett has overseen the creative direction for brands such as Vans and *Pica~Post*.

POSTER FOR SUN ARAW at Soup Kitchen. Digital and handmade collage, 2015

Opposite: BOOK COVER FOR *WONDER ROOM #1*
by Steve Hockett. Screen-printed collage, 2013

POSTER FOR BILL KOULIGAS. Digital and handmade collage, 2014

POSTER FOR STOP MAKING SENSE. Digital and handmade collage, 2013

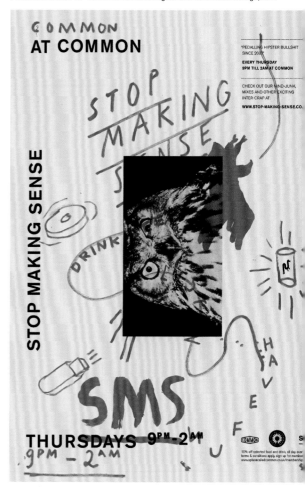

When did you first come across collage?
I remember being really into Kurt Schwitters when I was pretty young.
That's my classy answer, but in reality it was probably covering my
school exercise books in cuttings from skateboarding magazines.

As well as Schwitters, whose work particularly stands out for you?
I really like Eric Copeland's record sleeves – his last few for Black
Dice are really great, and the imagery works so well with the music.
Gore, the book he and the band did with Jason Frank Rothernberg,
is also amazing.

What attracts you to the medium of collage?
I use it in my design practice because a lot of the time there isn't one
available image to work with, so you have to make something up. As my
illustrations are pretty terrible, I use whatever I can find that will fit. I
like the colours and textures you get from reusing old print, and I also
like the idea of recontextualizing imagery, making it say something new.
I'd tell you it's ethical to recycle, too, but maybe I'm just being a bit lazy ...

Do you prefer to make collages digitally or by hand?
It's better by hand; I do work digitally but I hate the infinite possibilities
it offers. I'm a bad decision maker, so if I'm doing something on a
computer I'll try loads of subtly different variations and not be able
to choose what's best. In fact, I'll probably pick the worst. When you're
working by hand you can just get on with the design and not be able
to undo it afterwards. I'll go with that ... much easier.

Have you ever used anything unusual in a collage?
Marshmallows. And toothpaste.

THE BEAUTY WITCH & GREY LANTERN PRESENT

FÖLLAKZOID

+DEAD SEA APES & JASON BOARDMAN (DJ) 7.30PM TUESDAY 2ND JUNE AT SOUP KITCHEN £8.50 SEETICKETS / WEGOTTICKETS

VILLAGE GREEN

Comprising six creatives, Village Green is a London-based graphic design studio whose clients range from global consumer brands (Nike, Becks, Sky and Universal Music) to celebrated arts institutions (Barbican, British Film Institute and Granta). Village Green's designs exhibit an overriding concern with the darkness of pagan rituals and folk traditions, consisting of, for example, sharp-nosed plague masks, disembodied mouths and eyes (see pages 276 and 278) or warped body parts and animals. However, they are also responsible for more commercially minded material, such as their sleeve artwork for Mark Ronson's album *Version*. The studio tends to assemble their collages from disparate elements, exploiting the juxtapositions between unrelated objects to create work that is often alarming or unsettling.

POSTER FOR FABRIC. Photographic collage, 2008

Opposite: POSTER FOR FABRIC. Photographic collage, 2008

When did you first come across collage?
[Paul Byrne from Village Green]: Each of us has a different relationship with the medium and we each engage with it in different ways at different times. As a studio, though, artists such as Roman Cieślewicz and Peter Phillips inspired us in the early days.

What attracts you to the medium of collage?
Collage combines design, craft, illustration and photography, and although you don't need to be a master of any of them, you do need a good eye for composition. There is a freedom to collage, and there is also something satisfying about the appropriation of images – disrupting and creating meaning.

From where do you source your original material?
By its very nature, collage allows you to find imagery from a wide range of sources. We often flit between taking our own photographs, finding objects around home or the studio, mark-making or taking imagery from old nature books, encyclopaedias and manuals.

Have you ever used anything unusual in a collage?
To name a few: jelly, an animal's head, a Sainsbury's plastic bag ... The Fabric posters offered a lot of opportunity for experimentation with some very odd elements.

Do you prefer to make your collages digitally or by hand?
Every job is different. As with our varied methods of sourcing imagery, we alternate between a manual and digital approach. In general everything ends up on the computer, though, as digital processes offer more scope – we have even started to work with CGI elements over the past few years. Having said that, there have been instances where we have made collages entirely by hand. Mark Ronson's record sleeves are good examples.

POSTER FOR FABRIC. Photographic collage, 2008

Opposite: POSTER FOR FABRIC. Photographic collage, 2008

YOKOLAND

The Norwegian design studio Yokoland does not stick to one particular method of creating collages, putting the focus on experimentation instead. As a result, their pieces always feel playful, humorous and human. Working with both digital and print formats, the studio is well known for its compositions for cultural institutions, book design and music packaging, with a list of clients that includes Domino Recording Company, *The New York Times* and Oslo School of Architecture and Design. Throughout, their aesthetic manages to be both idyllic and poetic without ever encroaching on mawkishness. Yokoland has received numerous design awards and, in 2006, they published their first monograph, simply entitled *Yokoland*.

UNTITLED, personal project. Handmade collage, 2006

UNTITLED, personal project. Handmade collage, 2006

When did you first come across collage?
[Aslak Gurholt from Yokoland]: I started making collages in high school. I did the first ones on my own, but then I began working collaboratively with Espen Friberg. At the time I don't think we really knew the difference between art, graphic design and illustration – we were simply trying out different ideas and techniques, which I think was a good starting point. Today little of my commissioned work would be categorized as collage, but I feel it's influenced the way I work quite a lot.

Do you prefer to make your collages digitally or by hand?
I don't prefer one to the other, but they each require different thought processes. For instance, with handmade pieces, I'm very careful not to change them later on or to make alterations on the computer. They feel too precious, like original pieces of art. I also like the limitations that you have when working by hand – there are fewer images to source and there is no room for implementing effects such as changing scale or colour. When I'm making a collage on the computer, it's a very different process and I'm much more open to changes. I'm not the kind of artist who constantly works with collage, with a studio that is filled with bits of paper. Most of my commissioned work involves book design, music packaging, creating identities for cultural institutions and other forms of graphic design. As a result, working with collage feels like a space free of deadlines and clients. Because I'm spending so much time in front of the computer I try to work by hand as much as possible, and I'm also careful about when to use it for commissions, since that might ruin the fun of it.

Is it this feeling of freedom that attracts you to the medium of collage?
One of the things that I like about it is the coincidental aspect. You can combine two images or pieces and get something completely new and different, or an idea that you wouldn't have come up with otherwise. I also like that I can't one hundred per cent control the size, proportions and colour. Compared to drawing, it's a very different way of working. Drawing requires you to think before you act and imagine what the end result will be. It's quite a slow process, or at least it is for me. Collaging is much faster – I can be more spontaneous and consider intuitively how different images relate to one another.

Before putting your collages together, where do you find your source material?
Photographic prints, books and magazines. Sometimes I also use plain-coloured paper or pieces of paper that I have painted. Since collaging is not something I do every day, the practice can often feel like taking up something that I once knew how to do. Consequently, I think the way in which I work with collage has changed naturally over time.

Which, out of all the works you have created, is your favourite?
I made a small collage some years ago from a postcard/photo of a ship [see left]. The only thing I did was to cut out the ship and tilt it slightly so that it looked like it was sinking. To begin with it wasn't really that important to me, but over the following years it gradually grew into something more significant and it struck me as one of the nicest things I had ever made. It was simpler than anything I had done previously ... maximum effect with as little effort as possible. I'm not even sure if it qualifies as a collage. To begin with, I gave it a title that was too poetic, so I changed it later to *Sinking Ship*. I like the work's simplicity and directness, and the idea that it's just a single piece of paper that's been slightly altered.

SINKING SHIP, personal project. Handmade collage, 2006

Opposite: POSTER FOR METRONOMICON MINI FESTIVAL.
Handmade collage, 2008

METRONOMICON AUDIO
MINIFESTIVAL   2008
TORSDAG 13. MARS
KL. 21.00
PÅ BLÅ
INNGANG: 100,-

LIVE:
CENTER OF THE UNIVERSE
KOPPEN
CYRANOARMAGEDDON
PILEMIL
ERGO
DJ EDB

ALBUM COVER FOR *PERHAPS INTERIOR HEART POLITENESS*
by Magnus Moriarty (Metronomicon Audio). Handmade collage, 2008

Opposite: LEAP INTO THE VOID,
personal project. Handmade collage, 2006

AGNES MONTGOMERY
AGNESMONTGOMERY.COM

ALIYAH HUSSAIN
ALIYAHHUSSAIN.CO.UK

ANNA BEAM
ANNABEAM.COM

ANNA PEAKER
ANNAPEAKER.CO.UK

ATELIER BINGO
ATELIER-BINGO.FR

BETH HOECKEL
BETHHOECKEL.COM

BILL KOULIGAS & KATHRYN POLITIS
P-A-N.ORG

BRÁULIO AMADO
BRAULIOAMADO.NET

CAMERON SEARCY
CAMERONSEARCY.COM

DAMIEN TRAN
DAMIENTRAN.COM

DR.ME
DR-ME.COM

ELLERY JAMES ROBERTS
LUH.XXX

HISHAM AKIRA BHAROOCHA
HUGOANDMARIE.COM/ARTISTS/HISHAM-AKIRA-BHAROOCHA

HORT
HORT.ORG.UK

HVASS&HANNIBAL
HVASSHANNIBAL.DK

INGE JACOBSEN
INGEJACOBSEN.COM

JELLE MARTENS
JELLEMARTENS.BE

JESSE DRAXLER
JESSEDRAXLER.COM

JOEL EVEY
JOELEVEY.COM

JOHN POWELL-JONES
JOHNPOWELL-JONES.CO.UK

JULES JULIEN
JULESJULIEN.COM

KUSTAA SAKSI
KUSTAASAKSI.COM

LEE NOBLE
LEE-NOBLE.COM

LEIF PODHAJSKÝ
LEIFPODHAJSKY.COM

LEWIS MCLEAN
LEWISMCLEAN.COM

LINDA LINKO
LINDALINKO.COM

LOUIS REITH
LOUISREITH.COM

MARIO HUGO
MARIOHUGO.COM

MAT MAITLAND
MATMAITLAND.COM

MATTHEW COOPER
MRCOOPER.CO.UK

MATTHEW CRAVEN
MATTHEWCRAVEN.COM

MERIJN HOS
MERIJNHOS.COM

MICHAEL HOLLAND
DISKONO.JIMDO.COM

MIKE PERRY
MIKEPERRYSTUDIO.COM

MIRKO BORSCHE
MIRKOBORSCHE.COM

MVM
THEMVM.COM

NARCSVILLE
NARCSVILLE.CO.UK

NEASDEN CONTROL CENTRE
NEASDENCONTROLCENTRE.COM

NICK MATTAN
NICKMATTAN.BE

NOUS VOUS
NOUSVOUS.EU

PAUL SAHRE
PAULSAHRE.COM

ROBERT BEATTY
ROBERTBEATTYART.COM

RONNY HUNGER
COMETSUBSTANCE.COM

SANTTU MUSTONEN
SANTTUMUSTONEN.COM

SEBASTIAN HASLAUER
HASIMACHTSACHEN.COM

STAHL R
STAHL-R.COM

STEFAN SAGMEISTER
SAGMEISTERWALSH.COM

STEVE HOCKETT
WONDER-ROOM.EU

VILLAGE GREEN
VILLAGEGREENSTUDIO.COM

YOKOLAND
YOKOLAND.COM

DR.ME, 365 from '365 Days of Collage' project. Handmade collage, 2015

A massive thank you to everyone who has helped make this book a reality – you know who you are and we couldn't have done it without you.

To everyone featured in the pages of this book, thank you for giving up your time and for allowing us to show your stunning work.

Ryan & Eddy
DR.ME

On the cover (front, inside flap, and back): Merijn Hos,
UNTITLED, for WeTransfer. Handmade and digital
collage, 2013

p.2: Ellery James Roberts, SINGLE COVER FOR 'WE BROS'
from the album *Go Tell Fire to the Mountain* by WU LYF.
Hand-cut collage, 2010

p.4: Mirko Borsche, UNTITLED, for *Super Paper*.
Hand-cut collage, 2013

p.7: Tsunehisa Kimura, TOSHI WA SAWAYAKANA ASA WO
MUKAERU (*The City Welcomes a Fresh Morning*) from *Kimura
Camera: Tsunehisa Kimura's Visual Scandals by Photomontage*
by Tsunehisa Kimura (Parco, 1979). Courtesy of the International
Institute of Social History, Amsterdam. © 2016 Estate of
Tsunehisa Kimura

First published in the United Kingdom in 2016 by
Thames & Hudson Ltd, 181A High Holborn, London WC1V 7QX

Reprinted 2021

British Library Cataloguing-in-Publication Data
A catalogue record for this book is available from
the British Library

ISBN 978-0-500-29224-2

Printed and bound in China by C&C Offset Printing Co Ltd

Be the first to know about our new releases,
exclusive content and author events by visiting
thamesandhudson.com
thamesandhudsonusa.com
thamesandhudson.com.au